PRAISE FOR *UNCOMMON GROUND*

"Loving engagement with folks with whom we disagree does not come easily for many of us with strong Christian convictions. Tim Keller and John Inazu are not only models for how to do this well, but in this fine book they have gathered wise conversation partners to offer much needed counsel on how to cultivate the spiritual virtues of humility, patience, and tolerance that are necessary for loving our neighbors in our increasingly pluralistic culture."

—RICHARD MOUW, PROFESSOR OF FAITH AND PUBLIC LIFE,
FULLER THEOLOGICAL SEMINARY

"For anyone struggling to engage well with others in an era of toxic conflict, this book provides a framework, steeped in humility, that is not only insightful but is readily actionable. I'm grateful for the vulnerability and wisdom offered by each of the twelve leaders who contributed to this book. The task of learning to love well—neighbors and enemies alike—is long and urgent, and it can be costly. And yet, as this book shows us, because it is the work of Jesus, we can pursue this love with great hope."

—GARY A. HAUGEN, FOUNDER AND CEO,
INTERNATIONAL JUSTICE MISSION

UNCOMMON
GROUND

CONTRIBUTORS

Claude Richard Alexander Jr. is senior pastor of The Park Church in Charlotte, North Carolina.

Rudy Carrasco is a program officer for the Murdock Charitable Trust and past board member of the Christian Community Development Association.

Sara Groves is a singer and songwriter.

Shirley V. Hoogstra is the president of the Council for Christian Colleges and Universities.

John Inazu is a professor of law and religion at Washington University in St. Louis.

Kristen Deede Johnson is a professor of theology and Christian formation at Western Theological Seminary.

Timothy Keller is the founding pastor of Redeemer Presbyterian Church in New York City.

Warren Kinghorn is a professor of psychiatry and theology at Duke University.

Lecrae is a recording artist, songwriter, and record producer.

Tom Lin is the president of InterVarsity Christian Fellowship.

Trillia Newbell is the director of community outreach for the Ethics and Religious Liberty Commission of the Southern Baptist Convention.

Tish Harrison Warren is an Anglican priest at Church of the Ascension in Pittsburgh, Pennsylvania.

UNCOMMON GROUND

LIVING FAITHFULLY IN A
WORLD OF DIFFERENCE

TIMOTHY KELLER
& JOHN INAZU

NELSON
BOOKS

An Imprint of Thomas Nelson

Published in Nashville, Tennessee, by Nelson Books, an imprint of Thomas Nelson. Nelson Books and Thomas Nelson are registered trademarks of HarperCollins Christian Publishing, Inc.

Thomas Nelson titles may be purchased in bulk for educational, business, fundraising, or sales promotional use. For information, please e-mail SpecialMarkets@ThomasNelson.com.

Unless otherwise noted, Scripture quotations are taken from New Revised Standard Version Bible. Copyright © 1989 National Council of the Churches of Christ in the United States of America. Used by permission. All rights reserved.

Scripture quotations marked THE MESSAGE are from *The Message*. Copyright © by Eugene H. Peterson 1993, 1994, 1995, 1996, 2000, 2001, 2002. Used by permission of NavPress. All rights reserved. Represented by Tyndale House Publishers, Inc.

Scripture quotations marked NASB are from New American Standard Bible®. Copyright © 1960, 1962, 1963, 1968, 1971, 1972, 1973, 1975, 1977, 1995 by The Lockman Foundation. Used by permission. (www.Lockman.org)

Any Internet addresses, phone numbers, or company or product information printed in this book are offered as a resource and are not intended in any way to be or to imply an endorsement by Thomas Nelson, nor does Thomas Nelson vouch for the existence, content, or services of these sites, phone numbers, companies, or products beyond the life of this book.

ISBN 978-1-4002-1960-5 (HC)
ISBN 978-1-4002-2107-3 (eBook)
ISBN 978-1-4002-2315-2 (ITPE)
ISBN 978-1-4002-2145-5 (TP)

Library of Congress Control Number: 2019952549

Printed in the United States of America

HB 08.07.2023

For Willie

Walk in a manner worthy of the calling with which you have been called, with all *humility* and gentleness, with *patience*, showing *tolerance* for one another in love.

CONTENTS

CONTENTS

INTRODUCTION

JOHN INAZU AND TIMOTHY KELLER

THIS BOOK'S CENTRAL QUESTION IS HOW CHRISTIANS CAN engage with those around us, while both respecting people whose beliefs differ from our own and maintaining our gospel confidence. The idea for this book grew out of correspondence we have had with each other over the past few years.[1] Both of us were exploring how people find common ground across deep and often painful differences. We wanted to learn how to provide a Christian response to the reality of our differences, or what scholars call "the fact of pluralism."[2] Too often, the fact of pluralism is obscured, at least in the United States, with idealized visions of "one nation, indivisible" and the pursuit of "a more perfect union." But our actual existence is often characterized more by difference and disagreement than by unity. Americans, like citizens of most Western nations today, lack agreement about the purpose of our country, the nature of the common good, and the meaning of human flourishing. These differences affect not only what we think but also *how* we think and see the world. This is the fact of pluralism today: deep and irresolvable differences over the things that matter most.

Understanding pluralism means understanding our past. The fact of pluralism is one reason the United States is not, and has never been, a thoroughly "Christian nation." To be sure, a white Protestant culture, or what in some circles is called Judeo-Christian culture, influenced this country's founders and shaped middle-class norms and values for much of its history. That shared culture—and its assumed consensus about public morality and the nature of religious practice—brought with it important social benefits, among them the building and sustaining of institutions and infrastructure. The vast majority of today's charitable sector—private colleges and universities, hospitals, and social service organizations—has its roots in Protestant (and later Catholic and Jewish) communities.

But this shared Protestant culture failed to recognize, and sometimes perpetuated, significant injustices. Protestants were often indifferent and sometimes hostile toward the religious freedom claims of religious minorities. White Protestants were largely absent from the civil rights movement, and some white Protestants engaged in personal and structural racism that exists to this day.[3] The social and legal power of the Protestant culture often stifled differing views about race, religion, gender, and sexuality.

Within this dominant Protestant culture, many Christians forgot the biblical counsel that on earth we have no lasting city (Heb. 13:14) and are not to place our trust in earthly princes (Ps. 146:3). Over the course of many generations, some Christians surrendered to the trappings of an earthly citizenship that obscured their deeper allegiances. While we are called to love our neighbors, our proper citizenship is in heaven (Phil. 3:20).[4]

Recently the assumed consensus of the Protestant culture has weakened, in part from a growing awareness of differences in religious (and increasingly, nonreligious) beliefs. At the same time, deep and accelerating social trends toward individualism and autonomy have eroded trust in social institutions: business, media, government, church, and even the family. Yet as Protestant culture has declined, no successor has appeared. Neither evangelicalism nor Roman Catholicism nor secularism has replaced the previous assumed consensus.[5]

This is the background against which we asked our questions about finding common *ground*, even when we don't agree on the common *good*.[6] We also wanted to explore how Christians might embody humility, patience, and tolerance, the civic practices that John identifies in his book *Confident Pluralism*.[7] We believe these embodied practices are fully consonant with a gospel witness in a deeply divided age. In fact, they not only make space for the gospel but also point, respectively, to the three Christian virtues of faith, hope, and love.[8]

The first of these practices, humility, recognizes that in a world of deep differences about fundamental issues, Christians and non-Christians alike are not always able to prove why they are right and others are wrong. Christians are able to exercise humility in public life because we recognize the limits of human reason, including our own, and because we know we have been saved by faith, not by our moral actions and goodness. That confident faith anchors our relationship with God, but it does not supply unwavering certainty in all matters.[9]

Patience encourages listening, understanding, and questioning. Patience with others may not always bridge ideological distance; we are unlikely to find agreement on all the difficult issues that divide us. But careful listening, sympathetic understanding, and thoughtful questioning can help us draw closer to others as we come to recognize the shared experiences that unite us and the different experiences that divide us. Christians can be patient with others because we place our hope in a story whose end is already known.[10]

Tolerance is a practical enduring of beliefs and practices that we do not share. It does not mean accepting those beliefs or approving those practices. In fact, the demand for acceptance is a philosophical impossibility. Every one of us holds views about important matters that others find clearly misguided. There is no way that anyone can embrace all the differing and mutually incompatible beliefs. But we can do the hard work of distinguishing people from ideas, of pursuing relationships with people created in God's image, while recognizing that we will not approve of all their beliefs or actions. Christians can demonstrate tolerance for others because our love of neighbor flows from our love of God, and our love of God is grounded in the truth of the gospel.

All three of these practices—humility, patience, and tolerance—demonstrate a principled empathy in which we speak "the truth in love" (Eph. 4:15). The ability to put ourselves in someone else's shoes requires humility, and the impetus for doing so requires patience rooted in hope and tolerance grounded in love. This is increasingly difficult at a time in which, as Sherry Turkle argues, social media and other technology significantly reduce our ability to exercise empathy.[11] Indeed, we have seen a sharp decline in our ability to sympathize, understand, and talk face-to-face with those who have different views and beliefs.

If our culture cannot form people who can speak with both conviction and empathy across deep differences, then it becomes even more important for the church to use its theological and spiritual resources to produce such people. The Christian calling is to be shaped and reshaped into people whose every thought and action is characterized by faith, hope, and love—and who then speak and act in the world with humility, patience, and tolerance.

In fact, when we are motivated by the love of Christ, we can do far more than simply tolerate. Think about your relationships with friends who hold beliefs different from yours. You don't just tolerate them. You laugh, cry, celebrate, and mourn with them. You risk a kind of personal vulnerability that requires more than just coexisting together in the same space. And what about those who overtly reject you or are even hostile to you? The answer is the same. Jesus doesn't tell us to tolerate our enemies. He says to love them. And thank God that Jesus does not merely tolerate us—he embraces us across difference and welcomes us into his arms.

The Plan of This Book

We have both spent a great deal of time writing, speaking, and thinking about how Christians can and should live in a world of difference. But rather than offer a series of prescriptions, we decided to offer stories—those of our own and of friends, old and new. We chose stories, knowing that narrative provides a kind of surplus of meaning, revealing and enriching our understanding in ways that a list of propositions, however clear, cannot. The writer Flannery O'Connor put it this way: "A story is a way to say something that can't be said any other way, and it takes every word in the story to say what the meaning is. You tell a story because a statement would be inadequate."[12]

The same God who revealed himself through stories created people who learn best through stories and the nuance and complexity that those stories capture. In this book you will find stories from people who occupy roles that many of us assume in relating to our friends, coworkers, and neighbors. We hope this approach encourages and equips you in your own engagement with the world today.

Part I explores the roles through which we *think* about our engagement with others. Kristen Deede Johnson reflects on the contribution of the theologian, and Tim Keller considers the role of the pastor. Tom Lin and Rudy Carrasco offer two different postures that Christians can assume: the adventurer and the entrepreneur. Part II looks at how we *speak* when we engage our neighbors in an increasingly pluralistic society. Tish Harrison Warren begins by reflecting on the role of the writer, which connects us to other people and shapes the world in which we live. Sara Groves, Lecrae, and John Inazu follow with chapters that examine how we communicate with others through songwriting, storytelling, and translating. Finally, Part III turns to how we *embody* our engagement with others. Shirley Hoogstra and Warren Kinghorn reflect on bridge building and caregiving. Trillia Newbell and Claude Alexander Jr. conclude the book by considering our roles as reconcilers and peacemakers.

You will find references in these pages to many of the issues that divide us, but no issue emerges more prominently than that of race. That is partly a function of the people we asked to contribute to this book. But more than that, we have found in speaking and writing to various Christian audiences that few issues have generated more controversy or required more understanding than those related to race. Moreover, we believe that few issues of social division today are more significant for the church and for society. Christians are unlikely to find a way forward in our pluralistic society without more honestly confronting the issues of race that divide us and the society around us.

The chapters in this book depict various parts of the body of Christ. But they also remind us that God engages with us by assuming each of these roles. In making himself known to humanity, God acts as theologian, pastor, adventurer, entrepreneur, writer, songwriter, storyteller, translator, bridge builder, caregiver, reconciler, and peacemaker.

The twelve authors of this book began our collaboration by gathering in person in St. Louis. We wanted to produce a work that reflected not only our individual contributions but also some of the goodness of working together and learning from one another. As we told stories around the table, we discovered shared longings and passions. We also discovered ways in which we experienced loss, pain, and isolation, both in our personal lives and through our engagement with others. At times, each of us has felt out of place—not only as Christians engaging in the world but also as participants in Christian communities engaging with fellow believers. We imagine that you may feel some of the same in your own lives.

We also saw in each other's stories the ways God uses other people to make us who we are. The chapters in this book are written by individuals, but these individuals were shaped through relationships with other people, other image bearers: mothers and fathers, friends, siblings, a high school English teacher, Yolanda, Granddaddy Bill, Eboo, Marcy, Batka. As we think of how to live faithfully in a world of difference, we realize that God does not leave us alone to do so.

Finally, we were reminded of the object of our confidence. Scripture tells us that faith is being sure of what we hope for and confident of what we do not see (Heb. 11:1). As Christians, our hope lies in the death and resurrection of Jesus Christ. We stake our lives on the surety of that hope and the confidence of that unseen reality. It is with that posture that we offer this book: a call to engage the world as we find it, doing so with confident hope rather than stifling anxiety. This does not mean that we will encounter an easy path or that the circumstances we confront will always offer reasons to celebrate. Much of what we find will be unfamiliar, unsettling, and ungodly. But some of it will be good.

Our engagement with the world will lead us into unfamiliar relationships and risky spaces. There can and will be costs. But we look to Jesus, who engaged the world, not just at the possible risk of his comfort but at the sure and certain cost of his life. "He has gone to be the guest of one who is a sinner," they murmured threateningly when Jesus went to the house of Zacchaeus (Luke 19:7), but he still went. "Jews do not share things in common with Samaritans," the apostle

John underscored in Jesus' encounter with the Samaritan woman
(John 4:9), but Jesus still spoke to the woman at the well. "Today you
will be with me in Paradise," Jesus told the thief on the cross (Luke
23:43), and he died. Through our confidence in the gospel and in the
Author and Perfecter of our faith, we seek to live as Jesus lived in a
world of difference.

PART ONE

FRAMING OUR ENGAGEMENT

THE THEOLOGIAN

KRISTEN DEEDE JOHNSON

I GREW UP NEAR WASHINGTON, DC, SURROUNDED BY POLITICS.
I helped with the campaign of a friend's father as he ran for state
office, watched our friendly county supervisor become a US congress-
man, and learned new insights in government class. When I became
a Christian and began to encounter questions like, "What does God
want you to do with your life?" I thought politics might be the answer.
So the summer after my first year in college, I headed into the city
with thousands of my peers to explore the world "inside the Beltway."

That summer I began to realize that my Christian convictions
and my political convictions were not particularly integrated. So I
started asking questions about how my life in Christ informed how I
think about our common life together—in politics and in the church.
Little did I know then that these questions would lead to a calling as a
theologian and a lifetime of theological reflection about how, in light
of the larger story of God's redemptive work and the identity and hope
we find in Christ, we might engage in political realities.

As I began this exploration of how my faith connected to politics, I was trying to make sense of what I experienced that summer
on Capitol Hill. As I attended intern events, I noticed a tone quite

different from what I had encountered in other settings: anger, anxiety, fear, a sense of embattlement in the face of active opposition, a drive to mobilize one's side. Baffled and concerned, I returned to my studies at the University of Virginia where I discovered professor of sociology and religion James Davison Hunter. Through my interactions with Hunter and his 1992 book *Culture Wars*, I found ways to make sense of my summer experiences and to further explore my questions related to faith and politics.

Hunter helped me see that underneath the political conflicts of the late 1980s and early 1990s lay differing systems of meaning and moral authority. On the surface were opposing political convictions about everything from what it meant to be a family to what constituted art; underneath those political disputes were competing and irreconcilable notions of the nature of reality, truth, and what it means to be a human being. Political actors did not necessarily recognize the existence of these deeper, animating layers, yet these dynamics were behind the conflict between those who wanted to "conserve" morals, truths, and ways of living from the past (conservatives) and those who wanted morals, truths, and ways of living to "progress" as times and knowledge changed (progressives). These two groups often acted as if they were at war over the future of America.

A crucial part of Hunter's argument was that this level of conflict was evident at elite institutional political levels (for example, within Congress and the nonprofits and lobbying organizations connected to Congress) but not in the culture at large. Hunter's work helped explain why, as an outsider, I felt jarred by the war-like language and atmosphere of the different events I attended on Capitol Hill. Things are different now. The conflict that Hunter diagnosed at elite levels is increasingly evident all around us. We can no longer imagine this conflict limited to certain pockets of our political life. Instead, it pervades our social media feeds, family relationships, and community interactions.

Even before this cultural conflict widened, as I continued to learn more about the nature of the political climate, reading about the breakdown of civil society and exploring the intellectual currents that were shaping culture, I became more concerned about the future of my country. I wondered whether we had the intellectual and moral resources needed to sustain the American experiment through the pluralism and deep divisions in our midst. These concerns helped propel me to attend graduate school to become a theologian.

Another part of my motivation to study theology was a passion for discipleship. My faith had come alive through a youth group that placed a strong emphasis on following Jesus as disciples. We met in discipleship groups, went on discipleship trips, and studied the life of Jesus with his disciples to learn more about what it meant to live as disciples and make disciples of others. And yet it didn't take long to recognize that it's not always easy to know what following Jesus looks like in a particular time and place. As I learned more about culture and its formative power while working as Hunter's research assistant, I found myself with even more questions about what it means to be a faithful disciple in the intellectual, cultural, and political realities of our day.

My call to become a theologian was shaped deeply by these questions of faith, politics, culture, and discipleship. I began this calling with questions and concerns about how faith shapes our political thinking, the prospects of the American experiment, and the state of discipleship within American Christianity. But as I learned more of what it means to be a theologian, I increasingly located these concerns within a larger theological framework of hope. This was not because the underlying problems dissipated, but because over time I was able to view our contemporary pluralistic context and our callings as disciples through a longer and more hopeful theological lens.

Learning from the Past

My theological guide on this journey was Augustine of Hippo. When I read Augustine's writings, I discovered that even though he lived hundreds of years before I did, he also wrestled with questions of faithfulness and pluralism. As I was trying to make sense of the relationship between Christianity and politics in a time when much in our culture seemed to be shifting, I learned Augustine had also lived through a tumultuous cultural and political period. I was encouraged by his wisdom and perspective as he wrestled with what those changes meant—both for Christians and for the larger world. Augustine helped me realize that the tensions and anxieties I had encountered in Washington were understandable responses to cultural change. At the same time, he reassured me that we are part of a long faith tradition that has survived tremendous political and cultural turmoil because our faith is rooted in Christ, not in any one political system.

Augustine was surrounded by a variety of religious convictions and cultural practices, many of which he explored before his conversion to Christianity in AD 386. In addition, he lived in a confusing political time. In a shocking turn of events, Rome—the eternal city, as it was known—was conquered in 410. Rome was a spiritually symbolic city within the Roman Empire, the first political regime to tolerate and ultimately embrace Christianity. Rome had played a formative role in the development of Western Christianity and was home to many Christians. The city's defeat and suffering at the hands of its conquerors confused both Christians and non-Christians alike. Many blamed

Christianity for the demise of the city, and Christians wondered how to live faithfully through this political upheaval.

To help Christians make sense of these unexpected political realities, Augustine drew on Scripture to argue that in this age before Christ's return, we find ourselves with two cities. One is the heavenly city, of which Christ is King and of which his followers are citizens (see, for example, Phil. 3:20; Eph. 2:19). This city is made possible by the saving work of Christ, who redeems and reorders our loves so that we can love God and serve others in love. The other city is the earthly city, marked not by love of God but by lust for power and domination. This city is a result of sin, which continues to manifest itself as people seek their own good over the good of others and use their power to dominate rather than to love and serve.

As Christians, our primary allegiance is to the heavenly city, not to the earthly city in which we live. In the earthly city, we are pilgrims, never fully at home, because our ultimate destination is the heavenly city. We ought not to expect to find ourselves at home in this age, nor ought we to expect the earthly city of which we are a part to embody our love of God. Our hope cannot lie in the earthly city but in Christ alone, who lives and reigns in and over all earthly realities and who will come again to fully usher in his kingdom.

Augustine's perspective helps us limit the hopes we place in any earthly political system, while reminding us that we have the strongest foundation for hope in Christ our King. Because of this hope, we no longer need to cling to the present age, its institutions, and its blessings as do those who only know citizenship in the earthly city. We can live through complex political turmoil without anxiety, trusting that God's redemptive work is bigger than a particular political arrangement.

Augustine's conviction is that Christians can live faithfully as citizens of the heavenly city in a wide range of political arrangements.

Christians are to follow the laws, customs, and institutions of the political societies in which they find themselves—provided that those laws, customs, and institutions do not hinder their worship of God. Ensuring the success of one particular political order is not, in Augustine's view, incumbent upon us as Christians. Political systems may come and go, but our citizenship in the heavenly city remains.

And yet, even as we take this big-picture approach to our citizenship, we are called to be involved in the earthly cities in which we live. The earthly city can achieve certain goods, and we as pilgrims can and should contribute to those goods, while recognizing that they are not the ultimate goods for which we were created and redeemed. Consider peace. The earthly city will never be marked by the peace that is only available in and through Christ, but nevertheless we share with citizens of the earthly city a desire for earthly peace. We can join them in seeking the earthly peace here and now. Here Augustine echoes Jeremiah's counsel to the exiles to seek the peace and prosperity of the city in which they lived (Jer. 29:7).

Looking back now, I can see even more clearly why I was drawn to the theology of Augustine. It's not that I believed his thought could be applied wholesale to the questions we are facing today in the church and in society. But the fruit of Augustine wrestling in his day provided biblical and theological concepts that could be instructive to us in our time. Here are some aspects of Augustine's perspective that I have found especially helpful:

- As Christians, we are called to contribute to the societies of which we are a part.
- As we do so, we ought to contribute to the good we share in common with all citizens, not just seek the good of Christians.

- We need to remember that this earthly city is not and never will be the heavenly city until Christ returns.
- Remembering the differences between the two cities limits our expectations for what can be accomplished in this earthly city, which will always be marked by lust for domination and power.
- We need to be discerning about where that lust for domination and power manifests itself, even among Christians.
- Our hope lies not in what we can accomplish here and now but in Christ the King, who is Lord of all. He reigns here and now, and he will come again to usher in the full peace and justice for which we long.

Living through tumultuous political times is hard. It brings out many questions, accusations, and anxieties. But as those whose hope is in the Lord, we can navigate these changes remembering that political arrangements come and go but Christ our King still reigns.

Learning to Be God's Family

In addition to these important lessons about my citizenship in the heavenly city, Augustine taught me that I had been very individualistic in my faith. Augustine could not have conceived of Christians who did not automatically view themselves as members of God's family. And as I looked more closely at the New Testament, I realized the biblical theme of citizenship in the kingdom of God through Christ connects to another equally significant biblical theme: becoming members of God's household as we are adopted into God's family (Eph. 2:19; Rom. 8:15–17). I had been a Christian for years without understanding this important theological truth. With a strong focus on personal salvation, my earliest faith communities helped me encounter God's saving, personal love for me. But as with many Christians of my generation, the faith into which I had initially been invited did not emphasize that when I came to know Christ I became a part of God's family in the church. I have since come to see that God's love invites me into a much bigger family than I had ever imagined.

As a result, I began to see that aspects of Jesus' teaching on discipleship that I had always taken on as a *personal* responsibility were more faithfully understood as part of a *corporate* calling. This didn't mean I lacked individual responsibility, but I no longer needed to think that everything rested on my shoulders. Whether in relation to being a disciple, making disciples of others, or seeking God's kingdom in the world, I had previously understood Paul's exhortation to make "the most of the time" (Eph. 5:16) as meaning I personally had to make everything happen. This was too much weight to bear, especially given all the challenges I saw within both the public realm and American Christianity. And it was hard to square with Jesus' teaching that his yoke is easy and his burden light (Matt. 11:30). My faith was transformed when I learned that the call to follow Christ was the call to follow him in community with others.

Another realization that transformed my faith was the understanding that Christ continues to live and reign in this world. The reality is not only that Jesus Christ died two thousand years ago for our sins, but that in his resurrection and ascension he has an ongoing ministry. Scripture tells us that Jesus "always *lives* to make intercession" (Heb. 7:25, emphasis mine) and that he "*is* seated at the right hand of the throne of the Majesty in the heavens" (Heb. 8:1, emphasis mine). As Jesus proclaims in Revelation: "I am . . . the living one. I was dead, and see, I am alive forever and ever" (Rev. 1:17–18).

These present tense verses matter. They show us that Jesus has an ongoing role in this world. The classic categories of Jesus Christ as prophet, priest, and king are helpful here. Christ continues to serve as prophet (through the witness of his life and his teachings entrusted to us in the Scriptures), priest (through his sacrifice on the cross and his ongoing intercession between us and God), and king (through his conquering of sin and evil and his unending rule at the right hand of the Father).

The ongoing ministry of Jesus Christ, made known and empowered by the Holy Spirit, means that it's not up to us to save others or save the world. We attest to the saving love of God in Christ, we seek God's kingdom vision for the world, and all the while we trust that God is active through his Holy Spirit. God is the one who calls, justifies, and sanctifies. And God is the one who will usher in his kingdom.

To put this differently, we are not called to be heroes who save the day or save the culture.[1] This is one of the key insights of Lecrae's chapter on storytelling. Our story is to live as beloved children of God set apart by the grace of God in Christ and the Spirit to seek the things of God. This changes everything about our posture as disciples. Neither the souls of other people nor the state of our cultural institutions is ultimately in our hands. And neither is our sainthood—our status before God as disciples—dependent on our work and striving. We are *already* beloved and holy children of God (Rom. 1:7; 1 Cor. 1:2; Gal. 4:4–7). Our motivation for seeking God's kingdom first comes not from the need to earn our way into God's family but from the adoption we have already received into God's family.

What this means is that ours is a family calling. As we respond to the call to live as Jesus' disciples and seek God's will in this world, we do so as members of God's family, sharing the calling together ("saints" is always plural in the New Testament, as Sam Wells reminds us) as we are empowered by the Holy Spirit.[2] It's an active calling, but not a cumbersome one: we are neither alone nor the individual agents of transformation. When I want to engage with the realities in my hometown, for example, I now understand that I don't have to tackle each problem I see by myself. I am part of a larger family of Christians. The members of my family are equipped in different ways to seek the peace of our city, and the head of our family, God himself, is actively making all things new.

And Yet . . .

And yet, these days our family does not always give people the best impression of the One whose name we bear. The painful divisions evident in my early exposure to politics have only deepened and become more entrenched. People with profoundly differing orientations toward how we understand truth, order lives, and structure family struggle to find common ground. In the midst of these culture wars, many Christians have placed unrealistic hopes in what can be accomplished through politics.

As James Davison Hunter has argued more recently, Christians in the latter decades of the twentieth century focused on politics as the best way to enact cultural change, dedicating much time, energy, and money toward that end.[3] It's not clear, however, that cultural change works the way those Christians assumed it did. Too often, they prioritized politics to the neglect of other formative cultural institutions and the callings of everyday Christians to engage in those institutions.

In the process, many of those who focused on political engagement became more shaped by the institution and dynamics of politics than they perhaps realized. The earthly city's lust for power is hard to escape, even with the best of intentions and motivations. Even the most well-meaning Christians were hard to distinguish from their counterparts when it came to the character of their political engagement.[4]

If we are indeed God's beloved children and saints called by God, then we need to ask: What behavior does the New Testament describe as fitting for God's family? Let's start with 1 Corinthians 13, which, as political scientist Amy Black has counseled, applies as much to politics as to any other area of life.[5] Paul challenged Christians to be known by their love, which he characterized this way:

Love is patient; love is kind; love is not envious or boastful or arrogant or rude. It does not insist on its own way; it is not irritable or resentful; it does not rejoice in wrongdoing, but rejoices in the truth. It bears all things, believes all things, hopes all things, endures all things. (vv. 4–7)

Galatians offers us another picture, in which Paul described those who live by the flesh as marked by such things as "enmities, strife, jealousy, anger, quarrels, dissensions, factions" in contrast to the children of God, who are to manifest the fruit of the Spirit: "love, joy, peace, patience, kindness, generosity, faithfulness, gentleness, and self-control" (5:20, 22–23).

Peter wrote similarly of what it means to be holy, noting that as God's "holy nation," as "aliens and exiles" in this world, Christians are to "abstain from the desires of the flesh" and by contrast, "conduct yourselves honorably among the Gentiles, so that, though they malign you as evildoers, they may see your honorable deeds and glorify God when he comes to judge" (1 Peter 2:9, 11, 12).

These passages do not preclude us from tackling difficult issues, making our differences of conviction known, or engaging in the hard work of politics. They do imply, however, that as we do so we have to attend to the character of our engagement. These verses make clear that as God's people we are called to be known not for resentment, anger, enmity, arrogance, or rudeness. Rather, honorable deeds, patience, kindness, generosity, faith, hope, and love: these befit God's family.

What does it look like for Christians to conduct ourselves honorably? I see John's call to confident pluralism as a way of living out Peter's admonition in our divided political culture. By the grace of God, we can be *patient* because we take the long perspective, knowing that Christ is, always has been, and always will be Lord, through many different political realities. We can be *humble* because, as members of God's family, we know we are entirely dependent on the grace and love of God extended to us in Christ, which we use to love others. We can *tolerate* those with whom we profoundly disagree because the love we have in Christ does not insist on its own way, but rather bears and endures all things as it waits for the day when we will see all things clearly and fully.

Three Biblical Images for the Journey

There are many ways to think theologically about our engagement as Christians in this particular political and cultural moment, marked as it is by pluralism, fracture, and change. But in doing so, I've found myself returning again and again to three particular biblical images: children, exiles, and trees.

Living as God's adopted children grounds us in his grace, reminds us that our identity lies first in who we are in Christ rather than in our political allegiance, helps us share the calling to seek first the kingdom of God with others in God's family, enables us to remember our dependence on God's active and ongoing ministry, and shapes the character of our engagement with others.

In addition, we learn from the Hebrew Scriptures that the people of God were often in exile, forcibly removed from their homeland. While in exile, they were permitted to grieve and lament that they were not yet home—that the world in which they found themselves did not acknowledge their God and was not designed to support their way of life. But they were not to give up their way of life or cease to acknowledge their God. Rather, they were called to remain and live distinctively as God's holy people (as evidenced by such things as their worship, their ways of eating and dressing, and their love of God and neighbor).

But neither were God's exiled people called by God to turn the nations in which they lived into Israel. They were not, for example, to try to establish Babylon as God's holy nation or to think that its laws or ways of life would reflect their convictions. Nor were they to abandon the places in which they found themselves. God did not call them to be so secluded as his holy people that they lacked concern for the cities where they were living or the peoples around them.

This was the tension God asked them to navigate: live as my holy people, as strangers exiled in a foreign land at the hands of the people living there, even as you seek the *shalom*, or welfare, of that place and those people.

Does it not seem that there are lessons here we could learn as we live out our discipleship in today's deeply divided society, where we Christians do not feel at home? What would it look like to seek the welfare of our earthly cities?

Here is where one final biblical image is instructive: trees. Among many other things, trees are known for their capacity to take in the potentially harmful gases surrounding them and offer life-giving oxygen to the world. Trees do not offer this oxygen only to their own kind; they improve the air quality for everyone. Of course, trees also offer many other benefits: beauty, shade, fruit, and a habitat for wildlife.

The world would be diminished in significant ways without the contributions of trees. Wouldn't it be amazing if that was our reputation as Christians today?

Not too long ago, I tried out the image of trees in a slightly different way in a decidedly pluralistic context. I had been asked by a group of prison inmates to speak at a conference they were organizing on restorative justice. The whole experience was transformative, from my correspondence with the inmate who invited me to the day spent with a packed audience drawn from many different backgrounds. This day-long gathering included former prisoners, spouses of inmates, parents of victims, department of corrections employees, college faculty, justice advocates who had been working to reform the criminal justice system, and Christian evangelists involved in prison ministry.

I had been invited to offer a Christian perspective on justice and hope, based on the book *The Justice Calling* that I wrote with my friend Bethany Hoang. I spoke about the ways that God's forgiveness in Christ gives us hope that perpetrators of injustice can experience redemption; then I connected it to some of the contemporary realities surrounding the criminal justice system and took questions. An angry hand shot into the air: How could I give such an exclusive account of justice and neglect all the other reasons people have for pursuing justice?

In my response, I turned to trees. My earliest scholarship on pluralism, I told her, had convinced me that we aren't more welcoming of differences when we water down each of our traditions, pretend they are all the same, or look only for common ground. Instead, we might imagine trees so deeply rooted that they have had the water and nutrients to grow wide branches—branches so wide that they overlap with other branches. We need those deep roots—the deep roots of our respective traditions, convictions, and practices—to fuel the growth of our branches in this world. It is as our branches grow that we might find places of overlap with others, who have their own deep roots. And as we find these overlaps, we might be able to work together toward common goals, even if animated by different reasons and convictions. To return to Augustine's language, we might be able to join together to seek the earthly goods we share in common.

~

As Christians today continue to try to make sense of our posture and our callings within this complex political and cultural moment, I hope and pray that we will not forget the timeless words of Scripture related to trees and their fruit and leaves. By God's grace, may we in the family of Christ reflect the descriptions found in these three passages as we seek to be like trees planted by streams of water in this particular time and place:

> They are like trees
>> planted by streams of water,
> which yield their fruit in its season,
>> and their leaves do not wither. (Ps. 1:3)

The fruit of the Spirit is love, joy, peace, patience, kindness, generosity, faithfulness, gentleness, and self-control. (Gal. 5:22–23)

The leaves of the tree are for the healing of the nations. (Rev. 22:2)

THE PASTOR

TIMOTHY KELLER

I GREW UP IN A LUTHERAN CHURCH IN SOUTHEASTERN Pennsylvania, as my Keller family forbears had for generations. When I arrived at Bucknell University, a young man who lived in my freshman dorm hall nagged me to attend a campus ministry group. Those in the group treated the Bible as authoritative over human reason, culture, and public opinion. They also believed that every person had to be converted or be spiritually lost, and that we could only be saved by grace through faith in the death and resurrection of Christ, not through our moral efforts. That was "the gospel." Christian faith could only be chosen; it could not be inherited.

Every one of these evangelical tenets diverged sharply from those held by the mainline Protestant church with which I was familiar. Nevertheless, the campus ministry group intrigued me and I began attending. However, I was unsure whether I wanted to be any kind of Christian at all.

Philosopher Charles Taylor has traced how Western culture moved from religion toward secularity. Previously, one's individual identity was worked out in relation to some higher sacred value or order. You only became a person of worth if you were "embedded in some larger whole," something more important than your individual needs and impulses. But after World War II, that changed in Western societies. Taylor called this new era the "Age of Authenticity." For the first time it was proposed that the individual self—not the family, tribe, or nation—was of paramount importance. Identity no longer came through submitting to one's duties in a community. The self could create its own truths and morality, and the society would have to adjust to *it*. Significance came not through our roles in society but through self-expression—through finding and achieving our "true" and "authentic" self.[1]

In college I was able to consider living without any Christian faith at all because I was developing what Taylor calls a modern "buffered self," an identity that did not feel the pull of higher, transcendent truths and powers.[2] Since my mid-teens I had been looking inwardly and saw desires to do things that did not fit with Christian doctrine or church practice. My ancestors would have sacrificed their internal feelings to external obligations, but I felt only a duty to my deepest dreams and inner wants.

The mainline Protestantism I knew in the 1960s offered a kind of compromise. It said it was possible to have an expressive self and still believe in Christianity. It was clear, for example, that in that kind of church you could be an active member and still have sex as desired. You could believe whatever Christian doctrines you found plausible and reject the others. You yourself, your intuitions and feelings— rather than the Bible or church teaching—were the final arbiters of right and wrong.

I faced three possibilities: abandon Christianity completely so that I would be free to pursue my desires, ambitions, and passions without any inhibition; reaffirm being a mainline Christian; or embrace the gospel and throw my lot in with the little, despised band of evangelical Christians on a very progressive campus.

Why did I end up choosing option three? Writing fifty years after the events, I cannot remember my thought processes perfectly. But one way the campus ministry group appealed to me was by claiming that their way was based on evidence and argument. Looking back on it, some of these claims were overblown, and yet this invitation to reason and to think, rather than to simply follow my desires, was compelling. Almost as decisive for me, however, was an unadorned reading of the gospel texts. Our fellowship meetings were largely Bible studies. As a group, we read the passages and discussed our observations. Without coercion, I discovered in those texts a Jesus who was inexplicable on the basis of my then-held theories about who he was. When reading the Gospels, I had a sense of personal encounter with an immediate presence, and yet the texts appealed to my reason as well. I concluded that the Jesus I met there could not have been fabricated by the early church, nor could he be domesticated as just another religious sage or teacher.

The Christian gospel confronted me, one could say, at the world-view level. It challenged the baseline narratives of my culture. If Jesus was who he said he was, then my identity was not something I could define by myself. I could only realize my true self by aligning with Christ. I reflected long and hard on Jesus' words in Mark 8:34–37, especially as they were rendered in the New English Bible translation:

> Anyone who wishes to be a follower of mine must leave self behind;
> he must take up his cross and come with me. . . . What does a man
> gain by winning the whole world at the cost of his true self?[3]

It was a striking paradox. In one sense, to follow Christ is to "leave self behind," that is, to no longer make self-definition and fulfillment one's chief concern but rather to live for Christ. And yet, Jesus said, this *is* the way to discover your true self. In fact, if you were merely to achieve your goals and fulfill all your wildest dreams, you would only succeed in becoming alienated from the man or woman you were meant to be. You can only become yourself if you do what you were created to do—to serve and obey God unconditionally, to love and rejoice in him above all other things. There could not be a more countercultural idea.

It dawned on me that becoming a Christian would provide the inward benefits and goods that a modern person would want—a relationship with God, an assurance of love and pardon, a hope for the future that could even face down death. Yet these goods come only by giving up the supposed freedom to pursue self-definition. Christianity meant, therefore, being forever out of step in a culture that teaches its members, "You are your own; you define your meaning and self." Instead, the message of Christianity was, "You are not your own . . . for you were bought with a price" (1 Cor. 6:19–20).

During my last semesters of college, I began to experience the challenges of being publicly identified as a Christian in a secular setting. To face this head-on I took a number of religion classes, all taught by either mainline liberal Protestants or atheists. Some instructors and students were more polite than others, but all of them expressed surprise that an educated person could come to the conclusions I was embracing. At least two professors sympathetically told me that if I didn't abandon my too-conservative convictions, there was no way to have any kind of academic career, or if I was thinking of the ministry, to serve in any kind of respectable church.

I have never been a combative person, and I frankly found these interactions to be intimidating. But despite the social pressures and the self-doubts, I came to the conclusion that the evidence and arguments were on the side of evangelical Christianity.

Becoming a Pastor within "Christendom"

By the end of college, I was not only a convinced Christian but I also wanted to go into the pastoral ministry. I went off to seminary where I met Kathy Kristy, whose spiritual pathway was largely similar to my own. Raised in Pittsburgh in a mainline Presbyterian church, Kathy came in high school and college to evangelical convictions about the authority of the Bible and the necessity of conversion. We married before graduating and moved to our first church, West Hopewell Presbyterian Church in Hopewell, Virginia.

In the mid-1970s, Hopewell was in no way a secular, pluralistic society like the one I had experienced during college. It was what could be called a "Christendom" society. According to one scholar, that meant "a society where there were close ties between the leaders of the church and those in positions of [cultural and state] power, where the laws purported to be based on Christian principles, and where . . . every member of society was assumed to be Christian."[4] That is, there was major social pressure put on people to go to church and a social cost if they did not. Small-town Virginia at that time certainly reflected this kind of Christendom. You might not get that promotion or get into that local club or get a mortgage at the local bank if you were not a churchgoer. That sort of social benefit was long gone in the Northeast, even in the 1970s, and on my college campus there had been not only no social benefit to being a Christian, there had been a social cost.

Hopewell, in contrast, had an entrenched, culturally conservative culture. Virtually everyone there was essentially born into the same evangelical beliefs that Kathy and I had only arrived at through much intellectual and spiritual effort, and in the face of opposition. Hopewell people held their beliefs much like many of the secular students and professors at Bucknell held theirs. All thought that their positions were obvious, that all intelligent people believed the same things, and that anyone who did not was beyond the pale.

There were other ways in which the supposedly Christian culture of the South was like the secular North. Our secular and mainline liberal friends shared support of civil rights for African Americans, which aligned with biblical teaching on justice and love of neighbor, but they also promoted sexual liberation, which did not.

The Christians of Hopewell, while loudly endorsing biblical sexual ethics, were highly resistant to the civil rights movement. Ironically, Hopewell churches were being influenced more by their surrounding conservative culture than by the Bible, just as the northern mainline churches were being influenced more by their liberal culture.

At some point, a major realization set in. Kathy and I began to see that the biblical, evangelical faith that had changed our lives was out of step, not merely with liberal society (which consisted of both secular people and mainline liberal church people) but with traditional, conservative culture as well. Long before most people spoke of blue states and red states, we began to see that the gospel was not the property of either camp. Paul's classic presentation of the Christian gospel in Romans began with a depiction of Gentile, pagan immorality in chapter 1. In chapter 2, he described Bible-believing, highly moral Jews. Then in chapters 3 and 4, he explained that both legalism (thinking you can merit salvation through moral effort) and antinomianism (thinking you can live as you please) are ways of looking to yourself for salvation instead of relying on the work of Jesus Christ. Week after week I would visit with people in Hopewell and ask them what hope they had of going to heaven. They all believed in heaven, and virtually all said, "I hope to go there because I've tried all my life to be a good person and live as a Christian." If Paul was right (and he certainly was!), then these folks were in many ways as alienated from the gospel of grace and an experience of God as our secular, liberal friends. In both instances, the results were similar. While one culture was seeing the decline of marriage and family, and a growing obsession with self-fulfillment and individual happiness, the other was filled with self-righteousness, bigotry, and abuse of power.

If we had never moved to the South from the more liberal, pluralistic culture of the North, we could have fallen into the error of thinking that Christianity was just another form of conservative traditionalism. We would not have seen that the gospel leads us to critique, sharply but humbly, both societies.

Not too long after we arrived in Hopewell, my younger brother, Billy, came out as gay to our family and moved to Baltimore to live with his partner. Billy concluded that he could not be both gay and a Christian. Nevertheless, he wanted to maintain a relationship with the Christians in his family, and we wanted the same with him. Our visits to Baltimore with Billy and his partner, Joaquin, threw into stark relief how the gospel stands over and critiques all cultures. Billy and Joaquin were thoroughly unconvinced of Christianity, and Joaquin was especially incredulous that intelligent people of goodwill could hold historic Christian doctrine and views of sexuality. At the same time, we knew many people in the evangelical, conservative, southern culture who simply would have nothing to do with gay people at all. One side wanted us to accept the dominant culture's beliefs about homosexuality, while the other wanted us to cut off homosexuals entirely. The Christian gospel, however, did not allow us to do either. The gospel did not fit the conventional categories or received perspective, and Christians who followed the gospel were out of step with everyone. Yet our understanding of the Christian faith did not allow us to disengage, caricature, or demonize anyone at all, either secular or traditional. Our understanding of ourselves as sinners saved by sheer grace made it hard to feel either disdainful or fearful of anyone.

Becoming a Pastor in the "Secular City"

Our family moved to New York City in 1989 to establish a new congregation, Redeemer Presbyterian Church. Even though I had been an ordained minister for nearly fifteen years, my pastoral ministry changed in significant ways when we arrived in the city. In Hopewell I had to convince churchgoing people that they did not understand the gospel and that they were somewhat like the Pharisees, the people of Romans 2. In many cases I had to challenge highly moral people to consider if they really knew Christ through his saving grace. I also had to show them that the gospel critiqued the cultural waters in which they swam and created a Christian counterculture. I wanted them to feel less at home in their society while serving and engaging it in the workplace and neighborhood, rather than merely condemning it.

Manhattan, however, was a secular, pluralistic society, much more so than my college campus in the late 1960s. Here I had to convince people who had rejected the faith that they, too, had never understood the gospel. They saw Christianity as just another form of moralism, of self-righteousness. They had turned away from something they had never understood. I had to argue with them that they were much like the people of Romans 1, seemingly irreligious, but with a sense of and a desire for God that was suppressed but could be discerned in their aspirations and practices. Also, within the church I had to convince people that the gospel critiqued *both* the conservative, traditional culture of the Bible Belt *and* the secular culture of Manhattan. Christians in New York City felt strongly pulled by the cultural crosswinds in one of two directions.

One crosswind pressed believers to assimilate and adapt too much to the individualism and relativism of the city. They went to church for inspiration but still slept with the people they were dating. They loved it when the Bible condemned racism but were uncomfortable when it taught that sexuality was not theirs to do with what they willed. And they never tried to convert anyone. On the surface, this approach seemed more liberated and open-minded compared to conservative cultures, but actually these believers had adopted a modern identity based on self-expression and self-definition. God was only brought in as an accessory to enable their fulfillment.

The other crosswind led believers to find ways of living almost completely within a Christian bubble, something that was possible in Manhattan after the late 1990s, when many evangelical young adults began to move there with other Gen-Xers and millennials.

As a pastor, I had to demonstrate that both strategies were wrong. The biblical metaphor of Christians as "salt" was helpful. In ancient times salt brought out the flavor of the meat, and it also preserved it from decay. When Jesus told his disciples that they were the "salt of the earth" (Matt. 5:13), he was talking not of the ground but of the world, of society. As salt must disperse into the meat to do its work, so Christians are not to stay closeted and withdrawn but are to fan out into the world to bring out the best in their particular society, while seeking to offset its worst tendencies.

In a secular society there are moral ideals—caring for the poor, pursuing justice for the powerless, and seeking the equality of every person—that Christians can promote for biblical reasons. Indeed, Christians have the enormous inner resources for self-giving and self-sacrifice necessary to work for peace and justice in a community. On the other hand, our highly individualistic culture is seeing the decline of marriage, the avoidance of parenthood, the breakdown of politics, greater incivility, and the inability to forgive and show respect to opponents.[5] Just as salt can only help the meat if it retains its saltiness, Jesus added that we can only help the world if we retain our integrity. That is, if salt has exactly the same chemical composition as the meat, it can't help the meat. And if Christians become just like everyone else in their society, they can't help that society. We can only love and benefit our culture if we are different from it, if we maintain a Christian identity rather than adopt a secular one.

Another helpful biblical metaphor is citizenship, which Kristen explores in her chapter. Paul wrote that our main citizenship is in heaven (Phil. 3:20–21), yet in the book of Acts he regularly referred to and relied on his Roman citizenship. This is something like what we see in Jeremiah 29, where the Jewish exiles, who were ultimately citizens of Jerusalem, were called by God to be the most excellent citizens of Babylon (vv. 4–7). Counterintuitively, Christians' security, love, joy, and boldness in having our "names . . . written in heaven" (Luke 10:20) should make us the most outgoing, self-sacrificial citizens of every earthly community.

Armed with these biblical themes, I turned to the two kinds of believers being blown by cultural winds, either toward assimilation or withdrawal. I tried to make the first group feel less at home in their society. They needed to see that their citizenship in the kingdom had to take precedence and make them sharply different from the rest of the city in the way they used sex, money, and power. The second group had to recognize that they were genuine citizens of New York, and I urged them to serve and engage in three ways: by being public with their faith in their relationships, by integrating their faith with their work, and by working for justice and compassion in their neighborhoods.

Living out this dual citizenship has become more difficult over the years. When I arrived in New York, evangelical Christians were seen as perplexing curiosities. Today, they are often seen as a sinister force.[6] The professional world of New York City operates on relationships and networks, so Christians here fear that being public about their faith could hurt them in multiple ways.

As the situation in center city New York becomes the norm elsewhere in the country, Christians will need a great deal of pastoral guidance, support, and training if they are going to be salt and light and live with dual citizenship.

Love Will Find a Way

In secular, pluralistic cultures, Christians often are afraid to talk about their beliefs because they don't know what to say. Pastors of believers in such places often feel they must fill their flock with intellectual content until their people feel competent to take on all objections and arguments. But intellectual arguments, while necessary, are not of first importance.

As noted in the introduction, John's book *Confident Pluralism* lays out three practices that make civility and peace possible in a pluralistic society. He calls them humility, tolerance, and patience. People should be humble rather than defensive, should seek to patiently persuade rather than coerce and marginalize, and should tolerate and respect rather than demonize. Some critics of John's book have pointed out that our cultural institutions no longer form people with these traits, and so such agents of civility and reconciliation will be scarce. That may or may not be true, but the church, using the gospel, can and must form people with these habits of the heart, including a fourth one: courage.

The gospel removes pride, probably the greatest barrier to a sensitive yet clear exchange of ideas. It tells us we are sinners saved only by God's grace, not because we are wiser or better than anyone. It tells us that we must never think we are beyond sin and the need for repentance and renewal. There's the humility we need.

The gospel removes cynicism and pessimism as well. It gives real hope that people's eyes can be opened and change can happen. If we look at anyone and say, "That person is not the kind of person who will *ever* see the truth," then we contradict the gospel teaching that there *is* no "kind of person" who sees the truth. "There is no one who seeks God," says Romans 3:11, and therefore our faith and understanding is only due to God's intervention. God can (and does) work with any kind of person. We should, therefore, never think anyone is beyond hope of change. That gives us the patience we need, grounded in hope.

The gospel removes indifference. In Matthew 5:43–47, Jesus told his disciples that, since God gives good things to all people—"the righteous and . . . the unrighteous"—we should love and welcome everyone. In 1 John 3:16, we are told that since Christ laid down his life for us, we should lay down our lives for others. For Christians, the uncomfortable question is this: If we have been loved despite our flaws, and if we have discovered the greatest thing in the world in Christ, how can we be either abrasive or quiet about it? That knowledge produces the tolerance, but more than that, it produces the love we need.

Lastly, the gospel removes fear. While we should be concerned to not needlessly offend people, the assurance of God's love and acceptance should give us the courage to face criticism and disapproval.

There are four habits of the heart, then, required for a peaceful, mutually beneficial exchange of ideas between people who are deeply different. The same four traits are also necessary for any fruitful sharing of the faith with nonbelievers. The four major reasons for evangelistic unfruitfulness are a *lack* of humility, of hope, of love, and of courage. The gospel supplies all these things, if it is truly believed, understood, and rejoiced in. Pastors need to teach, apply, sing, and pray the gospel into hearts until these habits and traits grow.

And then what? Certainly Christians need instruction and training in the Bible and theology, and in answering the objections of skeptics. But if first and foremost the gospel of humility, patience, love, and courage is growing in you, well, love always finds a way. Think about just a few of the innumerable blessings we have in Christ: a satisfaction not based on changing circumstances; a meaning in life that suffering can't take away; an identity that is not fragile or crushing because it is not based on the ups and downs of your performance; a hope in the future that can face anything confidently, even and especially death; the ability to give and receive forgiveness and reconciliation; the inward resources for self-sacrifice that doing justice requires. How can we keep such things to ourselves?

Someone will certainly ask, "But what if we engage people around us with humility, patience, love, and courage, but they respond with anger, vitriol, and efforts to marginalize us?" The answer is that we don't take this path because we know it will be successful but because it is right. The psalmist, living in a land of exile, lamented that he lived "among those who hate peace. I am for peace; but when I speak, they are for war" (Ps. 120:6–7). There is no indication that he should give up and go to war; instead, Jesus told us to bless those who curse us (Matt. 5:44).[7]

Ultimately, pastors in the secular city do not need to be intellectuals who are constantly running sophisticated seminars on how to navigate our culture. If we use the simple means of grace—preaching and teaching, prayer, worship, the sacraments, fellowship, and friendship—to fan the flames of gospel faith in the heart, then a love for people and joy in the Lord will grow and overcome fear. And Christians will figure out how to reach out to others. Love born of God's grace will find a way.

THE ADVENTURER

TOM LIN

"ARE WE THERE YET?"

"Just a little farther," my dad replied, as always. "Be patient."

Even so, I leaned forward in the back seat of our red Pontiac station wagon, as if by force of will I could make us go a little faster. Peering between the front seat headrests, I searched for any sign that we were getting closer to our destination. We'd had only a short lunch break at a roadside picnic table, where my mom broke out the kimbap and stir-fry noodles before we were quickly back on the road.

It was our annual camping vacation, a chance to leave home with just a few clothes, a water cooler, a Coleman propane stove, and our tents. At that point in my life, it felt like an adventure into the wilderness. My brother and I hiked and explored, imagining we were the first people to walk those paths, far from the comforts of our home. We relished roughing it in the tents, with just a thin layer of polyester between us and the elements. We savored the simple flavors of camp food, so different from the Taiwanese feasts we ate every day. Before long, I asked again, "Are we there yet?"

I have always loved leaving home for an adventure.

I suppose this love for adventure runs in the family. My parents,

Sheng-Tsai and Sheue-Shua Lin, are Taiwanese immigrants. As young adults, they left behind familiar food, friends, and family for a country whose cuisine and culture, language and lifestyle, values and vision would always feel a little foreign. As a result of their adventurous spirit, I am the citizen of a country where the names Lewis and Clark, Armstrong, and Aldrin capture something fundamental about who we hope to be.

I am also the spiritual child of Abram and Sarai and Moses and Zipporah. And I follow in the footsteps of missionaries like Hudson and Maria Taylor and John and Betty Stam—people who left their homes and sojourned to distant places in response to God's call. People whose adventures transformed them.

The stories of Christians who have followed God's call to the adventure of missions have shaped who I am and how I engage the world. Their stories can also help Christians today navigate uncertain terrain closer to home.

Every Real Adventure Begins with Uncertainty

Camping always felt a bit risky to my brother and me when we were growing up. We were in the woods, far from home, and not too close to help. It would have been dangerous had it not been for my parents, who planned our trip, prepared our supplies, drove us there, set us up, and supervised our exploration. Or the government, which paved the roads, positioned emergency services within manageable distances, and maintained the park system. Or the backup plans that ensured, in the case of inclement weather, we could pile into the car and find a hotel. Our great adventure was really just a carefully orchestrated family vacation. And maybe that's why we loved it so much: it *felt* risky even though it was perfectly safe.

I wonder if the disorientation and dismay that some Christians experience today reflect what happens when people who have only experienced family camping trips find themselves in a real wilderness. Perhaps their desire has been like mine as a child on vacation: they want "adventure" and "risk" in an environment of safety. But the environment no longer feels safe. The culture, law, and politics that seemingly nurtured an evangelical resurgence from the 1950s to the 1990s have changed. Christians are not often affirmed or applauded. Instead, we are at times viewed with distrust or disdain as our divisions, hypocrisies, and failures have become public. We no longer feel at home and are unprepared for the real rigors and risks of being off the grid. We are unsettled by places where the paths are not well-trod, by situations where the safety net has been withdrawn, by difficult settings where the plans end and improvisation begins.

Are we lost? Should we despair? Or might God be inviting us to travel off the grid, to an adventure that exposes us to risks and possibly to transformation? Perhaps he desires for us to see the changes around us as opportunities that allow the church to grow in courage, faithfulness, and resilience. Perhaps he calls us to mature in faith that reflects confidence and trust in the triune God.

If that is what is happening, how do we accept the invitation? First, I think, by paying attention to our "entry posture"—the mindset from which we approach our new location or a changing culture. We can choose to be suspicious, critical, prejudiced, and closed, or we can be open, accepting, trusting, and adaptable. Our entry posture influences how we'll respond when we experience the inevitable frustration and dissonance that new situations present. And it predicts how we will emerge from the encounter—whether we'll experience alienation and broken relationships or deeper understanding and enduring relationships. Adventurers intentionally choose the posture of openness. When we expect the landscape to be challenging, we respond with nimbleness. Barriers become opportunities for creativity. Expressed hostility offers an opportunity to grow in empathy. The unexpected becomes an occasion for experimentation.

As I returned one summer from our family camping trip and entered first grade, I encountered a new adventure. As one of only two minority students in my grade, my context no longer felt safe. I found myself in the wilderness of a new school. In the uncertainty of new relationships and cultural differences, I viewed my classmates with suspicion. I feared how others would perceive my Asian appearance and did not want to risk explaining my identity or helping others understand. And when the inevitable question arose during that first week—"Tom, what are you? Where are you *from?*"—I responded without hesitation: "I'm Hawaiian."

My ambivalence and apprehension about my racial identity continued into college. As a freshman at Harvard University, I was disturbed by the lack of Asian Americans in the Christian fellowships on campus. *Where are my people?* I thought. *Why aren't they benefiting from the amazing experience I'm having in Scripture, community, and outreach? Who is looking out for them?* The otherwise vibrant (and largely white) Christian groups seemed oblivious. The few Asian American Christians I knew also seemed indifferent. The secular Asian American community seemed closed. I was troubled, and I saw an opportunity for an adventure. One campus ministry affirmed the dissonance I was feeling and encouraged me to ask questions and to initiate new programs to reach more Asian Americans. I stepped away from existing structures built largely for white students and entered new communities. I experimented with new ministry tools. I failed frequently and embarrassed myself often. But I saw the seeds of a new fellowship being planted, a fellowship that recently celebrated its twenty-fifth anniversary, where scores of alumni told stories of how God met them and transformed them at Harvard. Cultural dissonance invited invention and provoked transformation.

Today, I still observe cultural dissonance on university campuses, but I am encouraged by how this student generation is responding to it. For example, InterVarsity's chapter at Washington University in St. Louis recently noticed the growth of nonreligious and atheist students. Rather than being fearful, the chapter saw this cultural dissonance as an opportunity. They believed that atheist students would be open to conversation and relationship. So one day the Christians knocked on the door of the Freethinkers Society's meeting and asked the atheists to join them for a weekend of community service in St. Louis. The atheists responded, "Sure! That sounds like an adventure!" As they worked alongside one another, they talked and listened. They built relationships as they shared their experiences. They grew in trust and respect. A few weeks later, the chapter heard a knock on the door of their weekly Bible study. It was members of the Freethinkers Society. "Can we do Bible study together?" they asked.

In the midst of today's uncertain and changing landscape, adventures invite us to a posture of embrace rather than fear.

Unanticipated Costs and Unanticipated Grace

Abram and Sarai also experienced cultural dissonance in their adventure. Their journey began with a call to leave everything behind: "Now the LORD said to Abram, 'Go from your country and your kindred and your father's house to the land that I will show you'" (Gen. 12:1). Every adventure begins by leaving the familiar behind. When we cling to the familiar, like short-term missionaries who bring their own toilet paper, granola bars, and personal entertainment devices, we become burdened by our baggage. Demanding the privilege, position, and affirmation that many Western Christians enjoyed decades ago keeps us looking back longingly; eventually, like Lot's wife, we become too petrified to move forward. We fail to engage with what lies ahead. But moving forward into less familiar terrain often comes with a cost.

I experienced this kind of cost with my parents. My mom and dad, who had endured the pains of immigration and the scars of racism, worked hard so that I would have a better future. As they hoped, I performed well in high school, garnering accolades for athletics and leadership. I was my class valedictorian and named one of the top twenty high school students nationwide by *USA Today*. As one of eight American students to receive an "Academic All-American" award by the M&M/Mars company, I was even featured in a popular teen magazine and on an ESPN television special. And then came the highest honor any Taiwanese parent could imagine: the Harvard acceptance letter. My future was secure. I was the model minority.

But when I arrived at Harvard, I heard Jesus' call to follow him in a new way. In a Bible study on Mark 10, I sensed the Lord say to me, *I have a mission for you, Tom. Go, sell everything you have and give to the poor, and you will have treasure in heaven. Then come, follow me.* I cannot describe the pain and disappointment on my parents' faces when I told them that I had decided to walk away from job opportunities with six-figure starting salaries to begin fundraising as a missionary with InterVarsity Christian Fellowship.

My parents were devastated. We talked, argued, and wept for several days. Finally, seeing my resolve, they got down on their knees and begged me, with their palms open, "Tom, our lives are in the palms of your hands. Please don't crush us." My mom's last words to me in that conversation were, "If you do this, I will kill myself."

My parents, whom I loved dearly, stopped communicating with me. It was painful. My phone calls went unanswered. My letters received no reply. Both of my parents entered into a severe depression but still would not speak to me. They stopped going to church and withdrew from their own community of friends.

My parents' silence and withdrawal lasted for years. Then, in 2001, just as my wife, Nancy, and I had begun discerning a new opportunity for missions, my mom was diagnosed with stage IV stomach cancer. God used this time of extraordinary pain to draw our family together. When my parents reached out to me, we didn't talk about my career, the next steps for Nancy and me, or the past. Instead, we focused on chemotherapy, weekly hospital visits, and daily pills. As we spent more time together, I wondered if God was opening a door to reconcile our relationship. I began praying for this opportunity more earnestly and more urgently.

In the months that followed, I saw God work in my parents' lives in extraordinary ways. They turned to him for help and mercy, and they asked for his forgiveness and restoration of their relationship with him. They began praying regularly, reading the Scriptures daily, and attending church whenever my mom had enough strength to make it. They also began reconciling with their friends as they shared the news of her cancer. After years of isolation, my parents began to experience the restoration of their community relationships.

The final restoration came with me. One evening during a two-week visit over Christmas, my mom called me over to the sofa where she was resting. Tears streamed down her cheeks, and she took hold of my hand and said, "Tommy, there's something I've been wanting to say to you for a long time now. I'm so sorry. I'm so sorry. I know I caused you so much pain in the past few years. I should have supported you and just loved you. I'm so sorry, Tommy. I love you, Tommy." I was stunned. But I also felt an overwhelming burden lifted in my heart. Prayers that I had prayed for many years had finally been answered. "I know, Mom, I know. I forgive you. I'm sorry, too, for the pain that I've caused you. And I love you too."

The healing between my mom and me continued into early 2002. Then one day Nancy and I invited my parents into our living room to share our future plans: we were going to plant a Christian student movement in Mongolia. As we began to talk, my heart was pounding in fear. We had avoided the topic of Mongolia ever since my mom's cancer surfaced, but because the Lord was calling us to leave for Mongolia that year, we longed to receive their blessing. We were afraid that they would once again feel abandoned.

After we shared what was on our hearts, my dad started crying and said, "I've been reflecting so much on my life this past year. I realized that all my dreams have come true. I came to this country, and God has given me a stable job, two wonderful sons, your mom, a house . . . Tommy, I want your dreams to come true too. So if God is calling you to Mongolia, then you should go."

I had been longing to hear these words for the last ten years. Words of acceptance. Support. Love. And then, only a month later, my mom died. God had brought restoration in his timing. And now, with the full blessing of my parents, Nancy and I felt free to embrace the call to an even grander adventure.

Traveling Lightly

Mongolia was a country with no known Christians before 1989, and the Bible had not been translated into Mongolian until 2000. The average Mongolian household income was less than $40 per month, and the average winter temperature was minus-forty degrees (with winters lasting from late September through April). The challenges were, to say the least, daunting. Yet with nothing but our three suit-cases, our backpacks, and our winter coats, we left our familiar friends and familiar culture behind and trekked halfway around the world.

Our time was not easy. I remember vividly a cold night in our apartment in Ulaanbaatar, when Nancy and I sobbed and huddled on the floor of our bathroom in the dark. The power was out again, but we barely noticed it amid an argument we were having. We missed home. We missed friends. We felt alone and alienated in every way. But God was transforming us from tourists into sojourners. We were experiencing real losses, taking real risks, and feeling real vulnerability. Stripped of everything familiar, we experienced the adventure on his terms, reliant on his provision, and dependent on his mercy. Nancy and I were forced to believe that what Jesus said to Paul (who minis-tered in similar contexts) was true for us as well: "My grace is sufficient for you, for power is made perfect in weakness" (2 Cor. 12:9).

I often wonder what Christians in the United States will need to leave behind in order to embrace the adventure God has before us. I wonder what God might be stripping away so we can cling, desperately and helplessly, only to him. How does the longing for power, privi-lege, and position freeze us in place? How do our financial resources, technological tools, and cultural arrogance insulate us from an honest encounter with God and with the world?

What might it look like for us to travel lightly today?

Embracing Humility

Nancy and I arrived in Mongolia in 2002, with the security of American passports and a well-resourced ministry. But we also expe-rienced new vulnerabilities: we were metaphorically blind, deaf, and voiceless (because we could not yet read or speak Mongolian); unskilled (because our suburban upbringing did not equip us to address the practical challenges of a mostly rural country); isolated (because our friendship networks were unavailable in those days before social media and easy internet access); and marginalized (because as foreigners we were frequently mocked, robbed, and scrutinized by the police). These vulnerabilities invited us to embrace new virtues. We discovered the truth of what Lesslie Newbigin prophetically wrote in the 1990s in his book *The Open Secret*:

> We are forced to do something that the Western churches have never had to do since the days of their own birth—to discover the form and substance of a missionary church in terms that are valid in a world that has rejected the power and the influence of the Western nations. Missions will no longer work along the stream of expanding Western power. . . . And in this situation we shall find that the New Testament speaks to us much more directly than does the nineteenth century [and its early Western missions movements] as we learn afresh what it means to bear witness to the gospel *from a position not of strength but of weakness.*[1]

Nancy and I lacked all the gifts and tools that Americans typically bring to their local and global adventures. We could not simply throw money at the problems we faced. We could not out-strategize, out-communicate, or out-mobilize the problems. We had nothing, and we did not like it. We were little more than children, asymmetrically dependent on local Mongolians; we needed them more than they needed us. That process of being humbled, however, made us open to authentic relationships and attentive to the ways we burdened those around us. It embedded us in a network of relationships, obligations, and opportunities. It demanded patience. It required humility. It catalyzed love.

We experienced all of these graces through friends like Batka, a Mongolian college student who came to faith through a summer English camp we hosted. Nancy and I were his teachers; we were missionaries who came for Mongolian students like him. But it was Batka who would teach us. We needed his truth-telling about Mongolian culture and about the ineffective American methods we employed. We needed his newfound love for Jesus, which spurred on our own faith. We needed his friendship, which taught us generosity and grace. Three years later, Batka asked me to preside over and speak at his wedding. We remain close friends to this day.

Our dependence on friends like Batka also erased much of the Western arrogance, impatience, and individualism that we unconsciously carried. Our humiliation saved us from the Messiah complex and cultural imperialism that so frequently pollutes Western missionary endeavors. We were being prepared to embrace the challenge articulated by Samuel Escobar in *The New Global Mission* to do "mission from below," in contrast to the pattern of the old Christendom that could be described as "mission from above"—from a position of military, cultural, financial, or technological power.[2]

When I think of ministering from below, I think of my father. He grew up in poverty in Taiwan. He came to the United States with almost nothing in his pockets and knowing little English. By many standards, he succeeded and achieved the American dream. But he never deceived himself into believing he worked harder or was more faithful than others. He knew that others who worked just as hard remained in poverty in Asia. Other immigrants with similar English skills never made it to the upper-middle class that he achieved. Others who emigrated from different countries experienced more explicit and damaging racism. My father knew that everything he had was a gift of God's grace. That made him generous to others, including other immigrants. It gave him love even when he was marginalized by his work colleagues and passed over for promotions. He did not have much of a voice in those contexts, but his life spoke. You could see and feel his humility and dependence on God. For these reasons, whenever I find myself on an adventure, I long to be known as the son of Sheng-Tsai Lin.

I also long to be known as a son of God. We worship a God who came into the world vulnerable. As a baby, he was dependent on Joseph for protection and on Mary for sustenance. He gladly received financial help from women like Mary Magdalene, Susanna, and Joanna (Luke 8:2–3). He received water from a Samaritan woman. He ate frequently at the table of Mary and Martha. He hoped for encouragement and companionship from his disciples at Gethsemane. This vulnerability, as much as his miracles and teaching, moved the earliest disciples from awe to love. And it modeled an ethic of cultural engagement that once changed an empire—and could do so again.

Traveling Together

Nancy and I went to Mongolia hoping at some point we would have something of value to offer the believers there. Eventually, we did, even as we also received much from our new Mongolian friends. Our ministry became a true partnership with local Mongolian believers, based on authentic relationships forged in our months of complete dependence on others. We came to see that we each had different but important skills and knowledge—and that all of it was part of God's mission in Mongolia.

One Saturday, Nancy and I took the morning off, while the

Mongolian student leaders, who were well-prepared to lead Bible studies in Mongolian and to engage with their non-Christian friends, were leading a retreat. Unexpectedly, our phone rang. "Come right away!" the leaders pleaded. "We need you." When we arrived, we discovered that they wanted Nancy and me for very different purposes. They pointed Nancy to a room full of intensely praying students and asked her to conduct an exorcism, knowing of her charismatic gifts. They sent me to a different room to play board games with other students. Evidently, we each had our own, specific contributions to make!

Our culture is full of examples of teams of diverse and mutually suspicious individuals discovering the unique, essential contribution each has to make: epic stories like *The Avengers* and *The Fellowship of the Ring*, historical examples like Lincoln's team of rivals and unexpected military victories, and personal, local stories that many of us know firsthand. When we recognize our need for interdependence, we see ourselves and others rightly: as people made in the image of God, with unique and valuable gifts. That posture invites us to take risks together. It exhorts us to celebrate the success of others instead of feeling threatened, because we know that all of our skills are important in God's kingdom. And it leads to deeper unity.

Imagine what could change if we embraced a true spirit of interdependence with others. Racism, homophobia, misogyny, and our apathy toward those who differ from us would dissipate as we affirm our need for one another and freely acknowledge our sins and wounds. True partnerships would emerge between churches in mission, particularly between financially well-resourced churches in the United States and spiritually vibrant churches in other countries. Authentic interfaith and intercultural conversations would take seriously our differences as well as our common areas of concern. We might look more human, and more like Jesus.

We see glimpses of the kingdom-advancing partnerships that can emerge from humility and interdependency. Several years ago, I was intrigued to see an advertisement in a Chinese newspaper featuring the logos of Wycliffe Bible Translators, Save the Children, UNICEF, and IKEA. Together, they were cosponsoring a language translation project that would produce education materials in the mother-tongue languages of ethnic minority children in China. Save the Children wanted to educate these children but needed linguistic expertise. Wycliffe had linguistic expertise but needed the government approval that UNICEF could obtain. UNICEF had launched a global initiative to lift minority communities out of poverty but needed experienced organizations who understood how to work with children. They all needed funding, and IKEA wanted to share generously and invest its profits back into local communities. As a result, the kingdom advanced through a unique partnership of a for-profit furniture store, an evangelical mission agency, and two international nongovernmental organizations!

My work with InterVarsity Christian Fellowship has shown me other examples. Recently, a large public university in California asked InterVarsity to run its welcome week for international students. The university recognized our cross-cultural expertise and ability to mobilize the local community. We recognized that serving the institution in this way would help us reach more incoming international students. Similarly, an NCAA Division I school asked InterVarsity to train their coaches and athletic department staff to lead students in discussions about racism and cross-cultural partnerships. They had watched InterVarsity students lead these discussions on their teams during Bible studies and longed for their coaching staff to be able to lead similar conversations during practice, which benefits the whole campus. InterVarsity, in turn, depended on many coaches, who had daily interactions with student athletes, to mentor and support the Christian students. Our dependence on one another led to kingdom-advancing collaboration.

Interdependence is not without challenges. It presses us to discern how far we can partner or identify with one another. For some Christians who trace their spiritual lineage by how they have distinguished themselves from other Christian traditions (which they perceive as less theologically accurate, missiologically motivated, or behaviorally consistent), partnership becomes particularly complicated. They are wary of theological compromise and impurity.

I was forced to wrestle with questions of interdependence in a new way in 2015, when I led the planning for Urbana, InterVarsity's sixteen-thousand-student, triennial world missions conference. As part of a day-long program focused on how Christians around the world respond to oppression, we invited a Bible expositor from Asia, a church planter from Iran, a campus ministry leader from Tunisia, and others to share from their own experiences. We also invited an African American worship leader from St. Louis to describe the experience of the black church in the United States under the oppression of racism. She focused on how the black church has turned to worship and prayer to withstand the destructive forces around it. During her message, she also critiqued the silence of the largely white evangelical church. And she spoke approvingly of the prophetic rebuke of that silence by African Americans, including some involved with the Black Lives Matter movement.

Prior to the conference, and anticipating some controversy, I had visited the Black Lives Matter website. I thought that surely Christians could agree with its affirmation of the black community's "contributions to this society, humanity, and resilience in the face of deadly oppression." And certainly, I assumed, we could share the goal of "collectively, lovingly and courageously working vigorously for freedom and justice for Black people and, by extension all people." Of course, I also found positions and statements on the website with which I disagreed, and I could not affirm every action taken under the movement's umbrella. But this would be true if I were to review the websites of many Christian ministries and churches. I was not expecting to find that I could fully embrace every position held by an explicitly non-Christian movement. However, I had hoped we could work together against the sin of racism in our country.

Not everyone saw it this way. I experienced angry criticism against my leadership from some Christians who applaud our stances on personal holiness but reject our call to address systemic injustice. Months later, when InterVarsity affirmed its commitment to historic Christian teaching on human sexuality, the criticism came the other way, from those who affirmed our commitment to address racial injustice but rejected our views on human sexuality. As an organization committed to embracing a biblical ethic that addresses both personal and social righteousness, InterVarsity straddles different communities with whom we do not fully agree.

To what extent can and should Christians partner or express solidarity with other organizations over issues of common conviction? I wondered. John Inazu addressed some of these thoughts in an essay, "Do Black Lives Matter to Evangelicals?" published in the *Washington Post*. He concluded with these words, which still seem right to me:

> Finding common ground does not mean endorsing every goal or every value of the people to whom we draw near. But it does mean drawing near. That is at the heart of the vision of what I have called "confident pluralism." That vision is a challenge to enter into the

reality of pluralism around us to find common ground. And we can do so out of a confidence in our own beliefs.[3]

Most of us partner with people, institutions, and movements that diverge in important respects from our core convictions. We are members of families, employees of businesses, and citizens of countries whose goals and aspirations are frequently sub-Christian. When those differences are unjust or evil, we need to distinguish ourselves from them. But where possible, we should gather near, identify common ground, and draw lines as sparingly as possible. Salt should not remain in the saltshaker. A lamp should not be placed under a bushel. Christians should not fail to affirm the good, true, and beautiful wherever we see it, even if it emerges from sources with whom we would otherwise disagree.

We need to travel together, even in our differences.

Living in the world means seeking common ground with people and pursuits that are not always gospel-centered. For the adventurer, this is welcome news, because it allows us to ask different questions. *What might God be doing in this situation? With what struggles can I empathize? What bridges can be built? Where might the kingdom of God be manifesting?*

This generosity of spirit emerges not out of naive optimism but out of confidence in God's sovereignty and mercy. It anticipates delight. It presses us from mere tolerance of the unfamiliar to humble appreciation of the unexpected. It makes us open to new experiences and new ideas. There is a place, certainly, for discernment and scriptural critique, but those should be voiced with humility and love. Some might argue that this posture exposes us to danger. It does. Adventure is inherently dangerous. We should not be cavalier about this reality.

What gives us hope and confidence on this adventure, however, is the trustworthiness of our guide.

Resilient in Our Failures

There will be times that we fail, of course. But for people prone to adventure, risk and failure are invitations to grow in *resiliency*. When I trained college students for short-term missions experiences, I would often tell them, "What you do here isn't important. It's what you do next." When they expressed their puzzlement, I would say, "No matter how careful you are and no matter how carefully you prepare, you will make a cross-cultural mistake on this trip. You will embarrass yourself and, potentially, offend our hosts."

The students usually would look mortified at this point. "I am less concerned with the mistake you have made. I am more concerned about what you will do next," I'd explain. "Will you withdraw in shame? Will you dismiss the offense? Will you blame yourselves?" I would pause there, watching the students identify with their reflexive tendencies.

"Or," I'd continue, "will you lean in? Will you ask questions to learn what went wrong? Will you apologize and offer restitution? Will you extend yourself grace? Will you see this as an opportunity to deepen the relationship, to choose to become vulnerable and dependent? It's not what you do, but what you do next that will be important."

For students who had always succeeded by doing the right things, thinking the right things, and saying the right things, my words were hard to hear. These students had avoided failure their entire lives. They had always found ways to mitigate difficulty. This was particularly true for Christians raised in a culture that sociologists Christian Smith and Melinda Lundquist Denton have labeled "moralistic therapeutic deism," one that fears discomfort and avoids failure.[4] As a result, many students then and now lack resilience—the ability to bounce back from failure.

How can we develop Christians with resilient faith? I believe churches in non-Western countries, in immigrant communities, and among people of color could disciple us in this area. They have demonstrated resilience for centuries. They offer us examples of what joyful witness looks like in the midst of social sanction and cultural oppression. They provide models of lament that cling tightly to Scripture and engage intimately with injustice and sin. They show us how to confront the principalities and powers clustered around sex, money, power, and other idols. They participate in global and local mission without access to significant financial resources. Expressing theology and mission from the "bottom up," they bless those who for far too long have been ministering from the top down.

A few years ago, I was at the national conference of the Nigerian Fellowship of Evangelical Students. Like any college ministry conference, students there worshiped passionately and engaged Scripture eagerly. But unlike most college conferences in the United States, the conference center was guarded by dozens of guards with machine guns who stood ready against possible terrorist attacks by militant Islamic forces. This is their normal ministry environment. Kenyan peers of theirs were killed in the 2015 terrorist attack against Christians at Garissa University. Their friends and family have been killed by Boko Haram. Over 1.5 million fellow Christians have been forced from their homes and are without food. Nevertheless, thousands of students accepted the call to intentionally move to the Muslim-dominated North, putting their livelihood and lives at risk. Thousands more embraced the challenge to move to closed countries in Asia to proclaim the gospel. What gave them resilience? Declaring, "We won't give in to fear. The gospel is worth sacrificing our lives," they understood the value of the gospel.

More recently, I traveled to Lebanon, Jordan, Israel, and Palestine to hear from Arab Christians. While there, I was reminded of the ways God has preserved a church for himself over the centuries. I heard many stories of the ways God miraculously calls Muslims to follow him today. I spent time getting to know and learning from Palestinian Christian leaders who help their people through deportations, military occupation, and international isolation. What gives them resilience? They understand God's power and sovereignty.

Domestically, I continue to be challenged by the ways that black and Hispanic churches here in the United States integrate justice and evangelism into their gospel witness. Their worship resonates with both lament and praise, deep hope and honest pain. These fellow believers have experienced systemic oppression, economic poverty, and continual dislocation. Frequently, their concerns are rejected or minimized by other Christians. They often must work creatively around resource limitations. What gives them resilience? They understand that the kingdom has come and is coming.

Transformed by Adventure

I love adventure because true adventure *changes* us. Escapades do not. The movies I watched growing up, like *Star Wars* and *Indiana Jones*, usually featured a self-sufficient hero who has nearly everything he (and in those days, it was almost always a he) needs: wits, stunning physical strength and dexterity, sufficient material resources, and a surprising ability with ancient or obscure languages. What he lacks, he takes. If he is dependent on a local individual, that is a problem to be solved, rather than an opportunity to be celebrated. When he returns home, he arrives unchanged and largely unscathed. As entertaining as those movies were, they were ultimately unsatisfying.

By contrast, in the most satisfying stories, the adventurer is changed. In *The Lord of the Rings*, the protagonist, Frodo, begins the story weak and powerless. He is dependent on everyone for everything—direction, protection, and provision. He is so powerless and vulnerable that he fails. His mission is accomplished in spite of him, not because of him. But the journey changes him. This is no escapade. He returns home transformed, so ennobled and so broken that he cannot stay. "I tried to save the Shire, and it has been saved," he says, "but not for me. It must often be so, Sam, when things are in danger: someone has to give them up, lose them, so that others may keep them."[5]

Like Frodo, if we accept the wilderness we find ourselves in and embrace the journey God has us on, we will not stay where we are. We will not be able to return to where we began. We need to embark on an adventure. With each other and with God.

"Are we there yet?"

"Just a little farther," the reply always comes. "Be patient."

THE ENTREPRENEUR

RUDY CARRASCO

MY MAGAZINE MOCK-UP WAS MISSING. I HAD LEFT IT ON MY office desk the night before, but that morning it was nowhere in sight. The mock-up was sixteen white sheets of paper, scotch-taped together, with blue ink scribbles and boxes and headlines. It was a raw prototype of the first issue of *Urban Family* magazine. This was the summer of 1991, and Dr. John Perkins, a missionary community developer and racial reconciler, had decided to address the persistent media negativity regarding the black community. His vision was a counterbalanced publication that offered a different and more hopeful lens to address social problems. I joined Perkins's team right out of college and within a year became *Urban Family*'s managing editor.

By noon that day, the mystery of the missing mock-up had been solved. Perkins had taken it from my desk for a meeting with friends and church leaders. I heard later that he had waved my mock-up around like a lightsaber as he pitched his vision for a national magazine, one that would showcase hope and solutions to urban challenges and show black people and other marginalized groups in a positive light.

Imagine my shock when someone who had been in that meeting sent us $100,000 a few weeks later. We learned that this gift had been spurred in part by the rough appearance of my taped mock-up. This donor told Perkins, "You're not going to get any readers by mimeographing and stapling. You need a proper color cover and design."

Perkins got the idea for *Urban Family* after watching movies like *Menace II Society*. He was disheartened by the overall portrayal of black people in popular media, which was exemplified by major investment in movies about the realities of gang life yet offered relatively little exposure for more uplifting fare. Instead of merely complaining, he decided to do something about this media portrayal. And though the magazine launched with professionalism, he indeed was ready to photocopy issues and distribute them by hand if that's what it took. When he encountered a problem, he looked for a solution rather than merely griping about it.

We did not call ourselves entrepreneurs, but that is what we were. We created something out of nothing to fill a unique void. We were black-owned and focused on hope and solutions. Within a year, although not yet profitable, we had a print run of fifteen thousand and significant advertising revenue. We were structured as a nonprofit and relied on donations from Perkins's extensive network of friends. Our salaries were low and our staff of five was small. We had nonprofit infrastructure already in place, including office space, phones, and computers. The magazine was a lean start-up—with solid reporting and visual presentation—making enough of an impact that *Christianity Today* optioned it for a year to assess its market feasibility.

As is sometimes the case with entrepreneurial efforts, a fluke of history amplified the timeliness of our start-up. The first issue of *Urban Family* was in the mail on April 29, 1992, just as Los Angeles announced the acquittals of four police officers who had been filmed beating a black motorist named Rodney King. The acquittals were followed by five days of civil unrest, which was watched around the world and resulted in 63 people killed, more than 2,300 injured, approximately 12,000 arrested, and over $1 billion in property damaged. Rodney King himself went on television during the unrest and asked, "Can't we all get along?" Meanwhile, the article titles in *Urban Family*'s inaugural issue presented similar, thought-provoking questions, including "Who Speaks for the Black Community?" and "Can Blacks and Whites Be Neighbors?" Racial tensions remained amplified for the next few years, not just in Los Angeles but across the country, and *Urban Family* gained a foothold among people desiring solutions and racial reconciliation.

One takeaway from my *Urban Family* experience was the power of entrepreneurial, grassroots actions to address social problems. Our team repeatedly reminded itself to do more than criticize, to go beyond simply highlighting the depth of a problem, and to propose and enact solutions. Perkins called it "taking responsibility for the problem," choosing to clean up a mess we had not made. I was along for the ride, not merely riding along: I opted in, made the problems my own, and worked for solutions, even though I often felt ill-equipped for the task at hand.

Sometimes life thrusts you into the role of an entrepreneur, whether you see yourself that way or not. Christians are often called into high-stakes situations for which we feel less than ready and that require practical responses. You may have experienced this in your own circumstances. Perhaps you spoke out on an issue, turned around, and saw people agreeing with your message and asking you what they needed to do next. You may have taken action on a problem and found people and organizations coming to you asking for help with their problem. Maybe you didn't sign up to be a leader in helping people take practical steps to address their own challenges, but now you feel a bit like Forrest Gump: you took off running one day because you felt like running, and now people follow your example and wait on your words.

There's a term for this: *reluctant entrepreneur*. We usually think of entrepreneurs as people who tackle challenges without feeling constrained by existing resources. In contrast, author Randy Otterbridge defines a reluctant entrepreneur as someone who moves past fears to take the first steps toward creating an enterprise.[1] Christian leaders may not always identify as entrepreneurs, but those called to challenging situations may well be reluctant entrepreneurs.

And they are all around us.

There are people like Fannie Lou Hamer, who seed movements with courageous action. Her 1964 testimony at the Democratic National Convention changed the course of black voting rights in America. Her involvement in voting rights led to activism to end poverty, and in 1969, she founded the Freedom Farm Cooperative as a community-based rural economic development project.

Others take action to meet long-standing, pressing needs. When Wayne Gordon, a youth worker by training, and his team at Lawndale Community Church in Chicago saw a need for affordable housing for church members and others, they launched Lawndale Christian Development Corporation with appropriate leadership that was from the community and had the professional skills. This initiative has developed more than $100 million in affordable housing through 2019.

I am encouraged by these examples because I am also a reluctant entrepreneur.

Since my time with *Urban Family*, I have experienced so many situations of reluctant entrepreneurship that I've developed a three-step set of sayings that gives me strength to take action:

1. Things fall apart.
2. *Se hace camino al andar* ("You make the road as you walk").
3. "I can do all things through [Christ] who strengthens me" (Phil. 4:13).

Things Fall Apart is the title of a book by Chinua Achebe that chronicles the main character's despair as his Nigerian community capitulates to the British colonial presence. I've always been struck by the pithy and poignant title. The world is broken, and whether we can understand what is happening or not, sometimes things just fall apart. We will all encounter this kind of brokenness in our lives. I take comfort in this saying whenever I encounter fresh brokenness. Yes, things fall apart, but that is not the final word.

"*Se hace camino al andar*" is a Spanish phrase. The realization that there may be no path, no plan, no role model, and no precedent for the course of action one must take can be demoralizing. The reluctant entrepreneur may experience a period of paralysis when faced with such a daunting task. But the counsel to "make the road as you walk" tells me that there is a path, however costly, that lies ahead.

"I can do all things through Christ who strengthens me" is a central tenet of Christian faith and a rallying cry for the reluctant entrepreneur. We are, after all, the people who believe a man rose from the dead. When faced with great challenges, with problems that seem to lack solutions, we can take heart that the same Spirit who created the earth out of nothing can guide us into and through these obstacles.

Over three decades of ministry experience, I've seen positive changes when I and others have reluctantly moved from fear to entrepreneurial first steps.

In 1994, I transitioned from *Urban Family* magazine to another ministry founded by Perkins called Harambee Christian Family Center. Harambee was an urban youth ministry committed to racial reconciliation. In the northwest Pasadena community where Harambee was located, and where I lived and served, our immediate challenge did not involve racial tensions between ethnic minorities and the white majority but rising tensions between African Americans and

Latinos. Mistrust grew as more Latinos moved into a community that was majority black in the 1980s. Black gangs and Latino gangs further divided the residents from one another.

Our team at Harambee asked how the power of the gospel could be made known amid these community dynamics. With entrepreneurial thinking, willingness to take calculated risks, and cognizance that we would need to create something out of nothing, my ministry partner, Derek, and I decided we needed to be living witnesses of the black-brown racial reconciliation we believed was possible.

Derek was a black leader raised in Mississippi. I was a Mexican American born in East Los Angeles. Together, we chose to live in the community we served, have our families share a home and a dinner table, and operate the ministry jointly with equal decision-making powers. This was a greater sacrifice for Derek, who was ten years my senior and much more experienced in urban ministry operations. Over the initial three years of our effort, we created a culture at Harambee where blacks and Latinos looked after the interests of one another, and we convinced many of our neighbors that we were serious about the gospel's power of reconciliation. It was much harder to convince our neighbors to take risks themselves and form deeper relationships across ethnic lines, but over time our influence resulted in uncommon relationships between people who didn't even speak the same language but would still invite one another to their events and homes.

Another circumstance that called for entrepreneurial action came in 1997. A group of youth leaders, including Derek and me, was eating breakfast at a Denny's Restaurant in Orange County and lamenting the lack of youth ministry resources designed for urban environments. We asked what-if and decided we would have to create such an event ourselves. We linked arms with Dr. Larry Acosta of the Hispanic Ministry Center in Santa Ana to develop a pilot event. We planned the event together, marketed it by communicating with our respective networks, and identified Azusa Pacific University as the event site. We had a small budget but thought that the idea could gain traction if only people could see a demonstration. That first year we had maybe a hundred urban youth workers—and it was fantastic. But it was also absolutely draining, at least for the Harambee team. Derek and I went to Larry to let him know it was too much for us to handle at that time, and we told him we would have no qualms—plus he would have our support—if he chose to take over the Urban Youth Workers Institute event. Larry seemed energized by the entire process and gladly accepted. And the rest is history. The Urban Youth Workers Institute continues today as the premier national urban youth workers training space.

Another entrepreneurial opportunity came in 2007, when Mike (not his real name) stood in the doorway of my office at Harambee and said, "I hear you have the best gang program in the city. I want to know what you're doing." This was news to me because we did not have a gang program. "Who told you that?" I asked. He said some people around the city of Pasadena told him that Harambee was effective in its outreach to gang-impacted youth, but mainly he had heard it from youth at the nearby middle school. These youth were in our Junior Staff program, which combined college-prep and discipleship activities with a paycheck for hours worked around the facility. That was the year our youth program director, Florence, came to me and said we needed to hire more youth. We had budgeted and fundraised to have twelve youth working part time during the school year, but she said many new young people were showing up who had heard about the jobs. They were not Christians and were wary about Harambee, but they wanted to be there. We learned that some of these young people had relatives in gangs and were at risk of following in their footsteps.

I asked Florence what she thought we should do, and she in turn asked me what we could do. I said I could double our fundraising efforts, but I was uncertain how quickly we could raise the needed funds. She said she could lower the average hours each youth worked and thus increase the number of junior staff. "Really?" I asked. That would drop the hours to an average of four hours per week, and I wasn't sure young people would come for so few hours. We were also already low on work assignments. "I guess they can all take turns cleaning the same bathroom, huh?" I said. She replied that she could make it work. And she did. That year's class of thirty young people was the most attentive, sincere, and respectful group of youth I saw come through the doors during my nineteen years at Harambee. And they never would have come our way had we not entrepreneurially responded to the increased youth traffic by deciding to increase the junior staff and figure out how to cover the costs afterward.

I have one more example to share. By 2013, I had moved my family to Grand Rapids, Michigan, to work for Partners Worldwide, a global Christian organization focused on ending poverty through business initiatives. My Partners Worldwide team was invited into a meeting with business leaders across Grand Rapids who had gathered to lament the death of a young black man whom a number of them knew.

During the discussion, a question arose about addressing unemployment among African American men, especially those with conviction histories. While that day's discussion focused on seeing these men as potential employees, my team knew there was also a need to help these men operate sustainable enterprises. Some men faced challenges finding employment; some didn't earn enough from their jobs and needed a side gig, such as light construction, handyman, restaurant work, or anything they could find; and others had interest in working for themselves.

Grand Rapids is a private business heaven in that there is a culture that encourages private enterprise and self-sufficiency, so there was immediate interest in the idea that entrepreneurship could address unemployment needs. But people also wanted proof that it could work. We didn't have any local examples of entrepreneurship that uniquely addressed the needs of our target population. There was a slew of business development programs, but many assumed significant education or formal business acumen. We anticipated working with some men who had not gone far academically, and who were not accustomed to thinking in business formalities, such as business plans, budgets and spreadsheets, marketing plans, and the minutiae of legal compliance.

So my team set out to find a program somewhere in the country that worked successfully with our target population. We found a group in Chattanooga, Tennessee, called LAUNCH that had created a curriculum and a methodology that spoke the language of business to people who were not yet formal businesspeople. Partners Worldwide helped bring the LAUNCH methodology to Grand Rapids. The approach met the needs of an audience much broader than underemployed men with conviction histories. Five years after the initial idea, more than three hundred people from Grand Rapids's highest unemployment areas had completed business training, were in extended business coaching, and had launched more than two hundred businesses.

Urban Family. Harambee. Urban Youth Workers Institute. Junior Staff program. Partners Worldwide. These are just five examples of efforts made to address social challenges with entrepreneurial thinking and initiatives. Taking action served powerful, practical purposes: we convinced others that solutions were possible, because they witnessed change occurring in real time.

Beyond the practical, there is a theological foundation for addressing daunting social challenges in entrepreneurial ways. As Tim notes in his chapter, Jesus calls each one of us to live out our faith—to be salt of the earth—in places that need God's light the most, places that will most likely require entrepreneurial effort on our part.

Dr. Anthony Bradley provides an illuminating perspective on the nature of this salt: it is a fertilizer. In a 2016 *Christianity Today* article, he cites the work of agriculturalists Eugene Deatrick and Robert Falk, who noted that the ancient world understood salt as fertilizer. Bradley adds that this understanding continues today. The Philippines Coconut Authority describes how salt "accelerates crop growth and development, increases crop yield . . . [and] farmers who fertilized with salt had a yield increase of 125 percent over underutilized coconuts."

The application for this understanding of salt as fertilizer, Bradley continues, is that Christians are called to go where nothing is growing right now and help bring new life. "Christians are not here to merely season or preserve the world from decay. The followers of Jesus Christ are sent on a mission to stimulate growth in the parts of the world that are barren, and to be mixed into the manure piles of the world so that God can use that fertilizer to bring new, virtuous life."[2]

I love Bradley's perspective because it helps me see what God was doing in the entrepreneurial efforts in which I've been involved. All I knew at those times was that something had to be done and that it was worth the risk. But now I see more clearly that when Christians respond in faith and choose to be entrepreneurial, we are fertilizing the world and bringing life to places that need it.

Fertilizer was needed in Pasadena in 2007. As a backdrop, when I arrived in the early 1990s, the community was undergoing a wave of gang-related violence. In 1991, the *Los Angeles Times* reported on a drive-by killing that took place two blocks from our Harambee ministry site and noted that a half-dozen such shootings over a two-week period left residents tense and frightened.[3] A similar cycle of gang violence in our Northwest Pasadena community took place in 2007.

By September of that year, ten gang-related killings had already taken place. The toll startled area residents, since in the three previous years, there was a total of thirteen gang-related killings. Police conservatively estimated that there were eleven gangs with about five hundred identified members operating in our area.[4]

Residents and local leaders were concerned that gang influence was increasing, and the Vision 20/20 Initiative sprang up to address the challenge. The initiative started in late 2007 as a response to a call to action by a Pasadena City councilmember, Jacque Robinson, and it quickly employed a violence prevention framework developed by Anthony Massengale, a local Christian leader who worked with gangs throughout Los Angeles County. The Vision 20/20 Initiative focused on gang prevention and intervention and was implemented by a multisector coalition that included police, community-based and faith-based organizations, and philanthropic, business, civic, and educational organizations.

Harambee opted into this coalition, but not before I weighed the impact that our involvement would have on our organization.

A strength of our involvement was that a collective group could arrive at solutions that had eluded a myriad of organizations working in their own silos. We had a number of young people and parents who were gang-involved or gang-at-risk, so any positive movement in this area would benefit them. The challenges we faced involved use of time and whether we would face a value drift. Time-use was an issue because community coalitions inevitably result in a seemingly endless series of meetings: regular meetings, follow-up meetings to do the work of the committee, meetings to get to know others around the coalition table, meetings with officials and funders to lobby for change or support of the initiative, and so on. The other challenge, value drift, arose because not all the groups around the table agreed with the Christian-focused mission of Harambee. Would our presence at the table be perceived by Harambee supporters as compromising our mission and values? At the same time, others around the table had concerns about Harambee's involvement. They knew about our discipleship programs for youth and partnerships with individuals across the political spectrum and with churches that did not have progressive political agendas.

Knowing the strengths and the challenges of being involved, our Harambee team and I were intentional about building trust. Harambee was one of a handful of faith-based organizations at the 20/20 Initiative that year, and many leaders around the table were appreciative of our support and later, I believe, referred Harambee to their networks. That's one reason why Mike, who wanted to know about our gang program, came to our door. Yes, the young people at the nearby middle school had told him about us, but I also believe that people at the 20/20 Initiative table told him to check out Harambee's work with gang-impacted youth.

The 20/20 Initiative developed a number of approaches to help gang-involved young men and women, including an apprenticeship program that provided trade jobs, and a significant by-product was the new relationships between organizations that did not often collaborate. When I think back on how Harambee was able to provide some "fertilizer" to this effort, two factors come to mind: proximity and unspoken messages.

Regarding proximity, being face-to-face with others allows us to go past what we may have heard about their viewpoints or personalities and get to know them on a personal level. Often, we find that we have more in common than we first thought. At the same time, people get to know us. Some around the 20/20 Initiative had heard of Harambee's faith-based approach and assumed we were only about proselytizing or getting people to join a church. These skeptics were happily surprised that we were committed to serving all people in our community, and that we were focused on solutions that benefited the common good, not just our faith sector.

In terms of unspoken messages, I'm referring to body language. Our body language sends messages that will either strengthen or undermine our ability to be fertilizer. In an effort as fragile as a coalition serving gang-impacted young people, we had to do all we could to build trust among the participants. Did we have real concern for the people around the table? Were we sincerely interested in what others had to say? Were we open to following a collaborative process? Folded arms, crossed legs, manner of posture—all of these convey something about how we feel about these questions. Equally as important, a self-examination of our body language can give us insight into our own motives and heart. At times I have read my own body language and found discomfort, which spurred questions for me to reflect upon: Why am I uncomfortable? What can I do about it? Is it the person, the idea, or some other factor? How am I communicating to others? Is there anything I need to do in response to what my body is telling me?

~

Being an entrepreneur means being willing to create something out of nothing. And being a reluctant entrepreneur means moving in that direction despite your fears and anxieties. We may at times be less than hopeful for the prospects of social peace, racial reconciliation, and expanded community goodwill. But we should remember that we can creatively address challenges in our communities because the God we serve is creative. He has made us in his image and has given us the capacity to rise to whatever work he gives us to do.

The times in which we live may call us to take uncomfortable, extraordinary actions. Rarely do we choose these circumstances. We often don't feel equipped for the task at hand. But whether we are faced with tensions in our community as we watch our church or denomination wrestle with the great social issues of our day, or we are called to support fellow believers as they are faithfully present in public spaces, we can rest confidently knowing that God's track record is to make a way for us that honors him and brings life.

PART TWO

COMMUNICATING OUR ENGAGEMENT

THE WRITER

TISH HARRISON WARREN

I AM SOMETIMES UNCOMFORTABLE CALLING MYSELF A WRITER.
Neither I nor anyone else can be "a writer" generically, nor speak on
behalf of "writers." Many of us write. We write plays or instruction
manuals, emails or novels, poems or fantasy, blogs or children's books,
mysteries or memoirs, philosophical monographs or chemistry text-
books. All of this is writing, and each is a different sort of craft. I am
only one sort of writer. I usually write what could be called popular
theology—theology for nonexperts. For all of us who write, our particular genre, purpose, and audience shape our work.

I also hesitate to call myself a writer because, to me, the term has
an air of the exotic and exhilarating. Being a writer carries in my mind
all the sexiness, coolness, and instability of a Hemingway or Kerouac.
Most people I know who write are ordinary mortals. We are not very
interesting. We do laundry and mow the grass. We hope we say things
well on paper. Sometimes we do. Sometimes we do not.

But the main reason I don't feel comfortable with the term *writer*
is because I never set out to be a writer. What I always wanted to be
was a pastor. When I was around fourteen years old, I sensed a call to
ministry and eventually walked the aisle in my Baptist church to, in

their words, "surrender my life to full-time Christian service." I gradu-
ated from college passionate about social and economic justice, wanting
to be what my campus ministry group called a "world changer." But
I had no idea how one went about changing the world. I went over-
seas to work with the poor and worked stateside with a church serving
immigrant children. I wandered through a series of aimless jobs in a
bookstore, a doctor's office, a drug rehab clinic, an organic food store,
an elementary school, and a nannying gig. I went to seminary and,
after that, worked for nearly a decade in campus ministry. And then I
became ordained as an Anglican priest.

It was during my five-year process of ordination that I slowly
found writing became a bigger and bigger part of my life. Much to my
astonishment, the vocation of writing found me as much as I found it.
I first began to understand myself as a writer in two simultaneous but
radically different contexts: in new love and in the crucible of conflict.

After years of hoping for a baby and facing infertility, one happy
fall morning I found out I was pregnant. Here began a generative
season in every sense; as my daughter grew inside me, words began to
pour out of me. I had long reveled in words, so on a whim, I signed
up for a graduate-level poetry class at a local college. That gathering of
professors and students of poetry was a confederation of word freaks;
we gloried in words each week, and I grew little by little in the craft of
language. I had no strategic career plan; I had no sense of where this
was going—I wrote simply for the joy of it.

Then I met Marcia. Middle-aged, recently widowed, her grief was
deep and fresh. Yet she glowed with vivacity and a love of life. She
became my mentor and my unlikely muse. Marcia was an editor for an
online magazine. Right after we met, I told her offhandedly how, during
a very dark season of our marriage, my husband and I began to practice
Sabbath-keeping and the practice helped transform our marriage. She

asked me to write about it for her publication. After I turned in my essay, she called me on the phone: "You have a voice! Keep writing. Keep writing. Keep writing." It meant a lot to me, but I was busy and about to have a baby, so I did not write often. But Marcia kept after me. She called me up every few months; we'd catch up, and she'd ask me to write. Until, eventually, thank God, I did. Soon more opportunities to write opened up for me. The more I wrote, the more opportunities arose.

This new season of writing and motherhood was exhilarating. Words burned brightly in me—I'd wake up at night unable to sleep again until I wrote. Sentences demanded to be written. Discovering that I could write and having an editor whom I trusted was thrilling. I was a woman falling in love—with new work, with a new baby, with new words, with new ways of noticing and interacting with myself and God and the world.

I wrote to understand, to notice and make sense of my life. I wrote to learn, to figure out what I think and believe. I wrote, at times, for the sheer beauty of it, to preserve a moment of passing radiance.

When we write, we participate in Adam and Eve's vocation in the garden: the vocation of naming. We give words to reality, and through our words we help shape reality. This vocation of naming, whether in essay, verse, or story, allows us to encounter a new and mysterious depth of relationship with the realities we name. These creative acts change how we experience the world—and they change us. The stories we tell, the poems we write, the arguments we make, spin the shape of our lives.

As I was falling in love with writing, I was also walking through a season of conflict and loss. For two years, in the midst of my ordination process, I also worked in campus ministry with graduate students and faculty at Vanderbilt University. Then one spring day in 2011, Vanderbilt's director of religious life told me that our standing as a campus ministry group was in jeopardy. We either had to drop our requirement that our student leaders affirm our doctrinal and purpose statement, or we would not be allowed to remain on campus.

During the previous school year, one student had claimed that he was kicked out of his Christian fraternity for being gay. Vanderbilt responded by forbidding any belief standards for those wanting to join or lead any campus group. Like most campus groups, mine welcomed anyone as a member. But we asked key student leaders—the executive council and small-group Bible study leaders—to affirm the group's doctrinal statement, which outlined broad Christian beliefs.

The administration viewed any sort of binding belief statement suspiciously. They thought that any requirement of doctrinal fidelity could be used as a Trojan horse to marginalize sexual minorities. Furthermore, administrators came to see exclusion for any reason as oppressive and invidious. In a closed-door meeting, I once asked a group of administrators if they truly thought it was fair to equate racial prejudice with asking Bible study leaders to affirm the resurrection. The vice chancellor replied, "Creedal discrimination is still discrimination."

This local campus conflict quickly escalated into a widely covered news story. National media showed up to interview anyone they could find to talk about the new "nondiscrimination" policy that threatened to remove religious organizations from campus. We soon found that some media distorted the complicated facts on the ground. The conflict at Vanderbilt became an easy trope. Depending on the ideology of the audience, this was a story about the liberal, secular university oppressing the meek and mild Christians on campus, or alternatively, about the bigoted and backward Christians getting their just desserts from the heroes of progress.

We started to see that if we did not tell our own story, our story would be told for us, and it would be misrepresented in half-truths and culture war outrage.

THE WRITER: TISH HARRISON WARREN

So I began to write.

My coworkers and I started a blog to keep our constituents, students, and the watching world updated on what was happening on campus. We decided to write collectively, without using individual names: we were writing as a community on behalf of a community.

Through our blog, and through essays I wrote in the campus newspaper, we tried to make a case for preserving a diversity of viewpoints and ideas on campus instead of flattening differences by stamping out creeds and religious communities.

That year on campus was exhausting and full of grief. The university had been a haven and home for my family before this controversy. My husband was finishing his PhD there and wanted to be a professor. Our experience of rejection was disorienting. Administrators compared us to white supremacists. They told us, "We do not want religious faith affecting good decisions on this campus." We were mocked and derided. We were also confused—the policy kept changing. We were on probation, then told we were no longer on probation. Our hopes would rise after a good meeting with an administrator; then two weeks later we would read in the news that the administration had doubled down on the policy. In the end, we were kicked off campus with fourteen other religious organizations, which collectively represented nearly 1,400 students. Through it all, I wrote.

That year I wrote, in part, to argue—to attempt to get at the truth of things. I wrote to engage in debate in a way that I hoped brought clarity and light in a dim and turbulent time. And during that year of controversy on campus I saw, in a new way, the power of words.

Early into the controversy, my supervisor in campus ministry charged our team to never say or write anything that we wouldn't say or write in front of the most hostile university administrator. We wanted to guard against unnecessary conflict. But beyond the pragmatic art of diplomacy, our supervisor reminded us that we were called to love others, so we needed to talk and write about those with whom we disagreed in terms they would recognize. The scriptural command to "Do to others as you would have them do to you" (Matt. 7:12) required us to use our words carefully and respectfully.

And here was the small miracle I found: the way we used words shaped us. Our supervisor's admonition to use words charitably shaped how we felt about the university and its administration—it actually made us *feel* more charity toward those with whom we disagreed, and it changed our understanding of what was happening. It was not easy to articulate in writing our differences with the administration in a way that honored what was best about the university. It would have been much easier, and more attention-getting, to write a scorched-earth takedown of liberal elites in the academy. Our more nuanced task was to disagree publicly and try, however fumbling and imperfectly, to use words and arguments that were truthful yet humble and that respected the dignity of those with whom we were arguing—to be people who spoke and wrote with conviction, but who resisted the short-lived sweetness of self-righteous vitriol. This task kept us on our toes and forced us to lean into the tension of trying to maintain meaningful relationships with those who rejected us.

We were trying to understand the best arguments of those with whom we deeply disagreed, and, at the same time, to voice our own convictions unapologetically. We wanted to find an alternative to either a kumbaya get-alongism or a screed-screeching militancy. By taking up my supervisor's challenge, we found that we were able to see our ideological enemy more sympathetically, more like we see ourselves: human, fallible, valuable in the eyes of God. Our words changed our hearts.

But that year I also bumped into the limit of words. I honestly believed that if I could make the right argument, quote the right authorities, change the narrative, challenge the categories—if I could *write* well enough—we could resolve our conflict. I thought that, in the end, finding the right words could rescue us. But I discovered that no amount of winsomeness or intellectual rigor or cultural engagement or nuance would be sufficient to bring about reconciliation. Words are never, in themselves, salvific. They cannot rescue us from misunderstanding or fear. They do not have the power to finally conquer our own propensity for smallness and selfishness, foolishness or shortsightedness.

As someone who loves words, even as I celebrate the beauty and power they hold, I am often reminded that they falter and fail. Without words, we will not change culture, we will not understand our own lives, we will not fully know or be known—but words alone will never be sufficient for the task.

As Christians, we use words knowing they help us only to the extent that they lead us to truth, and ultimately to the Word, who was before all words and who judges and redeems all things—even our own glorious and unruly, luminescent and limited, little words.

Writing as Heralding

The Word—the Logos—is what the apostle (and writer!) John called Jesus. He is the Word of God, the language that brought everything that is into existence. The Word gives us words—earthen tools that help birth Beethoven's Mass in C Major and Rilke's poetry and Sunday crosswords and IKEA catalogs. When we take up the craft of these earthy words, we dare to participate in the redemptive work of the Word.

In seminary, a professor told me that my particular call was to herald. I had no idea at the time that this would involve writing. But since I've spent more days in the craft of words, that image has come back to me often. A herald is not the rescuer or the deliverer and is almost never the hero of the story. A herald's words do not actually save anyone. Rather, a herald's job is to be a messenger, to proclaim someone and something else.

Heralds are stock characters—archetypes—in literature. In J. K. Rowling's Harry Potter series, Hagrid is the herald; his arrival announces that reality is nothing like Harry thought and a new story is about to begin. In "Cinderella," the herald carried an invitation to the ball. In ancient Greek mythology, Hermes was the herald of the gods. In ancient Rome, a herald would come into town to announce a new king or a new law or an important event—a royal wedding, a battle won, an enemy defeated. Heralds announce a new reality.

Writers seek to proclaim truthfully what is and what can be. Christian writers are heralds; we understand our task as heralding the new reality of the kingdom of God—the wedding feast of the Lamb, a battle won through resurrection, death defeated. We herald that another reality has crashed into our own. We announce the end of the story. We whisper, speak, shout—in sentence and verse—that all things are wrecked and all things will be made new.

Our message—our gospel—is not always stated directly. Sometimes we convey our message apologetically or argumentatively. But we also, in the words of Emily Dickinson, "tell it slant," through a story well told, through a sonnet, through metaphor or just the right turn of phrase. When I doubt the story of Christianity, I read N. T. Wright's apologetic work on the resurrection. But when I really doubt it, I read Scott Cairns's poetry or Annie Dillard's description of a weasel's skull or Luci Shaw's verses about the sea. These writers tempt me to believe that the universe holds beauty, tragedy, and mystery far deeper and richer than I can now taste, that God might not only be real but also wildly, unrestrainedly at work in the world.

Heralding in Context

As Christians and writers, we herald a message. But, importantly, we do so in a particular moment in history, in a limited and received language, in a context, to a given audience. The gospel—which itself transcends time, space, language, and culture—is heralded, written, and received in the clunky and sometimes awkward gift of enculturated, time-bound, and ephemeral words.

The act of heralding always involves using the words that are at hand to proclaim something greater than one's self. It seeks to hold divine treasure in earthen vessels. Therefore, heralding not only involves knowing and proclaiming a message but also knowing and understanding one's own given moment in place and time.

Simone Weil is widely quoted as saying, "To be always relevant we must say eternal things."[1] And we have to learn how to say these eternal things—the dignity and worth of creatures, the brokenness at the root of humanity, the unrelenting redemption of God, the glorious newness that beckons us—in a language and voice that might make sense of them amid the particular confusion, conflict, longings, and limitations of our own brief era and place. To be a herald is not only to learn to say a message but to learn to speak it contextually and improvisationally, in the right way, at the right time.

Part of being a herald as a Christian is to speak hard—even unpopular—truths, eternal things that do not change according to culture and that offend, in one way or another, every culture. But we cannot simply speak uncomfortable truths in order to be right or, worse, to be primly pleased with ourselves. Our task is, in part, to communicate to others a meaningful vision of human flourishing—a way to know God—that makes people long for it to be true. This does not mean that all of our listeners or readers will accept our message, but if they reject it, we want them to reject something that we convey accurately. Like Jesus with the rich young ruler, we must be willing for our listeners and readers to walk away sad, but we must work hard to ensure that if they reject our ideas, it's because of the actual message we bear, not because we've bungled it into something unrecognizable and untrue.

I think of The Dude in the 1998 movie *The Big Lebowski*, responding to his friend Walter's overly zealous arguments: "Walter, you're not wrong. You're just an a**hole." The goal of a herald is never simply to be heard or to be right. Christians can use words in ways that are accurate but obnoxious or true but trite. But if we do so, we do not simply fail to be kind; we also fail to herald the kingdom of God. Because the eternal things we herald are not just ideas that, like math equations, can be recited and affirmed cognitively or propositionally. We proclaim a holistic vision of reality, of what it means to be human, what it means to live well, what it means to know God. We proclaim this vision in writing, in stories and sentences, and in our lives—with both our words and our practices.

Crucially, our words shape our practices, just as practices shape our words. Our task of naming things is a way to take up the practice of truth telling. And this task teaches us not just to *name* reality truthfully but also to *live* reality truthfully. This intentional practice of, in the words of Luci Shaw, "telling and retelling the story that weaves together divine transcendence and earthy human experience" shapes us as believers, and it shapes our readers.[2] As I have learned from the work of Stanley Hauerwas, the lies we tell tell us.[3] And the truth we tell tells us. Our words, our arguments, our practices of civility and restraint, our habits of word craft and speech work back on us to shape who we are, how we think, and what we are capable of saying in and to our world.

Words today are ubiquitous in a way we have never before seen in human history. Billboards, texts, tweets, posts surround us. Since the advent of the smart phone, most of us carry an entire world of glowing words in our pocket.

And this constant access to innumerable words can lead us to see them as both too important and not important enough.

On one hand, we give too much weight to words. We confuse the pursuit of justice—the slow work of building or transforming institutions and systems—with using the right hashtag or rattling off an opinion on social media or venting rage or virtue signaling. It's not that hashtagging or using social media are irredeemable practices. But social media is never a neutral tool; it shapes how we see the world—and how we speak and act in it. Ironically, it can lead us to greater disengagement even as we consume more and more information about the world. We can become too quick to speak or write, and too slow to listen, understand, and respond with depth and creative action.

The omnipresence of words can also cheapen them and render them weightless. Now, with blogs and social media, almost anyone can be a published writer, on any subject, with the simple stroke of a key. Mass communication is constantly at our fingertips, and with it comes a temptation to rush too quickly to respond—in public, with words—to any and every event. All of us, each day, every moment, can be buried under the weight of thousands of hot takes. But in the midst of an abundance of words, we can lose our care with words; we can lose meaningful argument and wisdom.

We now know that the internet is changing our neural pathways—the ubiquity of words online is actually rewiring our brains to take in small snatches of information quickly and forfeit the capacity to follow long, nuanced arguments and stories. This tsunami of words and information makes it more difficult to think and write well. And it produces incivility and tribalism. Nicholas Carr wrote, "We are accustomed to giving surface attention to things rather than depth attention—once I was a scuba diver in the sea of words. Now I zip along the surface like a guy on a jet ski."[4]

In response, we as writers can seek to cultivate depth. One way we do this is to practice—perhaps counterintuitively—patient silence and listening. We must cultivate attentiveness, to listen deeply to others, to our own interior life, to the great tradition of the church, to God. Thomas Merton said that "if preaching is not born of silence, it is a waste of time."[5] The same goes for writing—or, for that matter, any use of words.

We can resist the impulse to respond to whatever is trending with breathless pace. We can work against the pre-prescribed molds in which cultural arguments are so easily trapped.

Writing is hard. It should be hard—that's how our ideas get better. Understanding the world takes silence, listening, and careful reflection. All of this takes time, patience, and practice.

We, as writers, must embrace confidence in our convictions, yet still remain humble, a difficult balance that Tim explores in his chapter. We sometimes pit humility and conviction against each other—we conflate the reality that we can be (and often are) wrong, with a kind of relativism that never states anything definitely. We conflate eschewing dogma and eschewing pride. But all of us have to land somewhere—we all bet our lives on some version of reality, of truth and morality. The goal of writers, like the goal we had as campus ministers at Vanderbilt, must be to state our convictions clearly and (not but!) humbly. We need to learn how to be people of conviction yet always remember that we are fallen—that even our writing is fallen. This reality should make us take up our pens—or laptops—with a decent amount of fear and trembling and an even stronger hope in God's mercy.

Reclaiming Words

The novelist and poet John Berger wrote, "For us to live and die properly, things have to be named properly. Let us reclaim our words."[6] Using words is no small task. This vocation of reclaiming words—of redeeming words—is part of Christ's new creation that echoes the naming we did in the garden. And this act of naming determines how we live and die. Words build the cairns that guide the course of what we believe and who we are. Because of this, we need help from our community—from the church—to use words well and truthfully, and we need accountability as writers.

Naming the world truthfully, with care, is a loving act. Through stories, argument, and metaphor, we can love our readers and help them live in ways that are more abundant, more attune to wonder, more just and thoughtful and sane. Part of the Christian writer's call to love in our era is to upset the easy categories of Left and Right, good guys and bad guys, black hats and white hats—the simplistic and self-satisfied labels that bog down our contemporary conversations. This is, as Lecrae writes in his chapter, the key to good storytelling— and, more generally, to good writing. Instead of overly tidy categories, we proclaim a common brokenness that affects all of humanity and all political systems and solutions, and yet we also proclaim a common value and dignity of all people. Francis Spufford wrote that "Christianity overspills the separate categories by which we conventionally understand the world now, insisting to an awkward degree on common ground." And he reminds us, "This is not very comfortable."[7]

Writers, like other artists, remind us that no matter what differences divide us, we share much in common. We all bleed. We hope and despair. We wait in darkness for dawn. We taste and touch and smell. We hold in common this planet that risks the audacity of pufferfish and lightning bugs, of puffins and penguins and coral reefs. We all die, and everyone we love and fail to love dies. We all live our lives, every minute, fragile and vulnerable. Writers remind us that we are alive, no thanks to ourselves, and this gift of life is given to us together, to live in this world of light and darkness together. All of us deeply human. All of us deeply afraid. All of us, even the best and worst of us, are much like the rest of us.

And, sadly, there will be times when we seek to love our readers and they don't love us back. Writing always involves risk. We and our work will receive criticism and critique, which is a good, albeit painful, and essential part of getting at the truth and also of becoming a better writer. But in this moment in history, to state anything at all can unleash not just needed response but vitriol that is unreasonable and ad hominem (and, at times, massive and viral).

To write lovingly will inevitably entail, with its many joys, some wounds, some suffering. If writing is to be an act of love, we will have to extend tolerance and charity to our critics, even those who attack us unfairly. If we seek to be faithful as Christian writers and leaders, we will be criticized in stereo—on the Right and the Left—and, at times, those in either direction will seek to co-opt our work for their own ends. Living and writing in this place of tension takes practice. We hone our craft. We learn in time and in community, through patient silence, listening, and prayer, to name the world truthfully, to herald our message, clearly and humbly.

I became a writer in the context of a new love and a disorienting conflict. And I continue to practice writing in a world so very full of love and loss—and of wonder and horror, joy and sorrow, peace and conflict. And in this beloved and beautiful, wayward and weeping world, we bear witness to the Word, who will have the final, glorious word.

THE SONGWRITER

SARA GROVES

I WAS RECENTLY WITH MY TEN-YEAR-OLD DAUGHTER, RUBY, for some mother-daughter time. As we were checking in with each other over pizza, I told her I had been invited to contribute to a book about being a Christ-follower in these days, and I wasn't quite sure how to go about that. "These days?!" she said with a knowing laugh. "Do you know what you're allowed to write about? Have you asked them what's appropriate?" "No, I don't think I have," I said. She sighed and put her hands on the table. "Okay." She was ready to problem-solve this with me.

"If you are going to talk about these days, you have to talk about technology. And you have to talk about President Trump, I mean . . ." She shook her head for a while and said seriously, "Racism. You'll need to talk about racism." Long pause. "Memes. Memes are a big deal, and slime. All of my friends have slime." She thought some more. "That's about all that's going on these days, but you better call these guys and find out what's appropriate."

For the last twenty years, I have been attempting to engage as a songwriter with the world in which I live. Like a theologian, pastor, or translator, a songwriter looks for language that will help us name our experiences and understand what we are feeling. Precise language is important, and I have chased it for years. But I see an additional invitation for the songwriter: the songwriter is invited to say it all. To bear witness to the whole range of human experience, including all of its tensions. A songwriter is invited to speak of lament, fear, banality, silence, injustice, justice, hope, wild adoration, beauty, love, passion, natural and supernatural things. A songwriter is called onto the scene not to make spiritual sense of it, or to answer for it, but simply to look around and cry out, "Oh my God! Look at this unfathomable beauty!" Or, "Oh my God! Look at this sh*t show!" This is what we see in the Psalms anyway.

Before I go any further, I want to acknowledge that much of the language I use to describe my life as a songwriter has come from my exemplars in the music and art world: music producer Charlie Peacock; his wife, author Andi Ashworth; and visual artist Mako Fujimura. They have left deposits with me—conversations, written words, lived examples—and I have carried those inspirations into my world, my music, my neighborhood. They have given me a context for confident engagement with culture through their definitions of the "generative life."[1]

In his book *Culture Care*, Mako asserts that culture is not a war to be won but a garden to be cultivated. In this beautiful reformation of ideas, he shifts us away from the concept of enemy and into the arms of nurture and creativity. "When we are generative, we draw on creativity to bring into being something fresh and life giving. . . . What is generative is the opposite of degrading or limiting. It is constructive, expansive, affirming, growing beyond a mindset of scarcity." Mako believes, as I have come to believe, that this is of utmost importance "in even the harshest environments where survival is at stake."[2]

This idea that we can be generative in the harshest environments was brought home to me in the story of Vedran Smailović, the Cellist of Sarajevo. It is a story that has been told many times, but I was not aware of it in 2003, when I was working on *The Other Side of Something* with Charlie. I was on the tail end of an identity/faith crisis that had me questioning the value of words and ideas and wondering if I should start over in a new, more hands-on career. *What is the point of songs and poetry?* I thought, *If I didn't pass out at the sight of blood, it would be nice to be a nurse, to give physical comfort and care with my own two hands.* I was expressing these ideas at the kitchen table with Charlie and Andi when he told me the story of the Cellist of Sarajevo. Smailović witnessed great sadness in his home country during the Bosnian War. After a stray bomb detonated among civilians waiting in a bread line, Smailović decided to play twenty-two concerts in honor of the lives lost that day. He donned a full tuxedo and played his cello in the middle of bomb craters and ruined buildings all over Bosnia. His beautiful protest became a mobilizing metaphor for me. It is easy to stand around a bombed-out crater and talk about the crater—how it got there, who's to blame for it, and all its particulars. It is much harder to step past the edge of it, down into the middle, and say or make or do something generative. In his book *A New Way to Be Human*, Charlie states,

> Here's what I've figured out for myself: My life is going to tell a story whether I try to or not. It's going to tell a story that says, This is what a follower of Jesus is, this is what he or she is interested in, this is what he or she believes and trusts, this is what he or she thinks is important.[3]

As I understand the story, Jesus left perfect community to step down into our bomb crater, to enter into suffering that wasn't his own, and to play a song—and what a song! Everyone around him wanted a march, a call to arms, and instead he played the most beautiful, true song ever heard! We don't have to be in a war-torn country to find bombed-out craters. Wherever I am, I can participate in the divine nature; I can partner with God in the renewal of all things; I can be a repairer of the breach. As a songwriter, I believe I begin that work by taking up this invitation to bear witness to the whole of the human experience and letting my one witness go up like a song in a bomb crater.

> *Sit with me and tell me once again*
> *Of the story that's been told us*
> *Of the power that will hold us*
> *Of the beauty, of the beauty*
> *And why it matters*
> *Speak to me until I understand*
> *Why our thinking and creating*
> *And our efforts of narrating*
> *About this beauty, oh this beauty*
> *How it matters.*[4]

Say It All: Tell Yourself the Truth

The best writing advice I ever received, the advice that has produced the most fruit in my work, was to not edit myself. By not editing, I don't mean avoiding all self-restraint, but rather saying the closest thing to what is true. Tell the truth—the whole, complex, messy, conflicted, unflattering truth.

Truth-telling can't begin with the question, "What am I supposed to say?" or even, "What is the *faithful* thing to say?" It begins with an experience and moves toward whatever flows out: confession, praise, naming, testifying. If we judge our thoughts before we even have a chance to experience them, we create a hostile environment where we can't access our true testimony.

Several years ago, I was working on a song loosely based on a friend who had made an impulsive choice that had hurt people. It reminded me of Esau, who sold his inheritance for a bowl of soup. The song was going to be about how the good things of life require a little commitment; the chorus, of course, was going to drive home the point that we should do the hard work of waiting for the good, eternal things in life. But this is not what we do—and this is not what *I* do—on a pretty regular basis.

The more I worked on the song, the more I could see my own belly full of soup. It took me seven years to figure out that I didn't need a didactic song telling me what I *should* do; I really needed a song that sat with Esau and me in our post-lunch remorse and admitted that it gets cold here on earth. I needed a space to recognize that I still sell my here-and-now kingdom over and over again, even when the future inheritance is infinitely better.

> *Oh the power of wounds left unattended*
> *Sold my kingdom for a lightning bolt*
> *Am I to blame for all that is upended*
> *Searching for a god that I can hold?*
> *Moving like a proton through a neutron sky*
> *Looking for my healing in every passerby*
> *Oh my inheritance for a bowl of soup*
> *Something warm and real in the space of you.*[5]

I have found it very hard to tell myself the truth. It takes humility, awareness, grace, and room to write and wrestle with unvarnished truth. I, too, often fall short of that goal and fail to express my unedited self. I almost always start a song with what I think I'm supposed to say, then work my way to something that is true.

Flannery O'Connor spoke to this beautifully in *Mystery and Manners*, a book of collected essays on the act of writing:

> The novelist is required to open his eyes on the world around him and look. If what he sees is not highly edifying, he is still required to look. Then he is required to reproduce, with words, what he sees. Now this is the first point at which the novelist who is a [Christian] may feel some friction between what he is supposed to do as a novelist and what he is to do as a [Christian], for what he sees at all times is fallen man perverted by false philosophies. Is he to reproduce this? Or is he to change what he sees and make it, instead of what it is, what in the light of faith he thinks it ought to be?[6]

In O'Connor's estimation, those who endeavor to tell the truth about what they see have prophetic vision: "The prophet is a realist of distances."[7] Prophets see the way things are in painful contrast to their knowledge of and belief in full reconciliation.

The psalmist clearly felt free to be a "realist of distances." He shared openly about his madness, shame, and fear and how messed up everything seemed to be. In Psalm 73, Asaph testified, "The wicked look pretty happy to me! They are fat and powerful and don't seem to have trouble like other men. I wash my hands all day long, keep my heart pure, and all I get is a punch in the face. Why am I trying to do good again?"[8]

I've had similar thoughts. Why am I knocking myself out trying to serve others and love well? Why am I trying to find a kind reply when my neighbor deals daily in insults? My neighbor goes to work to make money and seems pretty fine with it. Do I really need to battle all day sorting out good and evil?

Because of all he saw, Asaph was confused: "I feel senseless, ignorant, like an animal."[9]

I don't know about you, but I feel less alone when I read this. I,
too, have felt like an ignorant, brute beast. And it is important that I
tell the truth about that.

It can be hard to go first—to be the first to confess inadequacies,
anger, confusion, fear—but I can attest to the fact that every time I
have taken that risk, it has been fruitful. Vulnerability begets vulnerability, and I have met listeners of all kinds who have found comfort
and freedom in the songs that were the hardest for me to write.

Say It All: Bear Witness

When I was writing songs for my fourth album, *The Other Side of
Something*, I felt compelled to write more about what I saw through
the lens of faith and less about the lens itself. I was struggling with
the culture of the contemporary Christian music industry and its
predictable need for lyrical clarity and certainty. I wanted to write
about real issues in my marriage and about the fact that while I said
I believed in change and transformation, I wasn't always experiencing it.

> *The butterfly can just look back*
> *Flap those wings and say oh yeah*
> *I never have to be a worm again . . .*

> *I am longing for something tangible*
> *Some kind of proof that there's been change in me . . .*
> *Change is slow and it fills me with such doubt.*[10]

It seems silly now, but it was a big deal for me to leave that lyric of doubt without a faithful bridge like *"but my butterfly days are coming, yeah."*

When I talked to Charlie about it, he said, "God is the ocean, and we keep writing about a cup of water!" He encouraged me to keep going, to write about all of it—what it means to be human, what incarnation can look like here on earth, and how far we can fall short of glory. A robust theology is an invitation to think through how everything matters.

If we bear witness to blessing but avoid lament, we lose credibility.

And there is so much to lament. Several years ago, I played at a fundraising event for an organization in Chicago that brings assistance to poor communities. Guests talked about red-lining, a historical practice where early city leaders determined (by literally drawing a red line on a map) where African Americans were allowed to live and not live.[11] This practice, coupled with brutal real estate inequities, meant little to no home ownership for African Americans. A man in his late fifties recounted to us through tears how his father, a successful doctor, was unable to get a mortgage for a house until 1978. When he explained that they lived two to three families to a house and still paid exorbitant rent, there were many deep nods around the room—this was a shared, common experience.

A few months later, I was in a class at church that is designed to bring me peace about my finances, and the teacher on the DVD instructed us to make sure that when we buy a house we find one on the "right side of the tracks." Afterward, my small group received my hot, teary lecture on how our city leaders had created the "right" and "wrong" sides of the tracks. The question burns in me: How do we as Christ-followers think about how we continue to participate in systemic inequities? What might I put in *that* bomb crater of injustice and grief?

Some hearts are built on a floodplain
Keeping one eye on the sky for rain
You work for the ground that gets washed away
When you live closer . . .
Closer to the danger and the rolling deep
Closer to the run and the losing streak
And what brings us to our knees
Some hearts are built on a floodplain.[12]

In Psalm 109, David wrote a song to God about a man he witnessed mistreating his neighbor: "For he did not remember to show kindness, but pursued the poor and needy and the brokenhearted to their death" (v. 16). David was grieved and angry, but he trusted God's heart for the oppressed. He closed the same chapter singing, "I will praise him in the midst of the throng. For he stands at the right hand of the needy, to save them from those who would condemn them to death" (vv. 30–31).

In 2005, I met a young woman who had been trafficked from her home to a country where she did not speak the language and where she was forced to work in a brothel. She was rescued in large part by the methodical, tireless work of the folks at International Justice Mission. Upon meeting her, I felt burdened to respond in a tangible way. I approached a friend in a flurry of emotion and said that I wanted to become a lawyer, or an aftercare worker, something more meaningful than a songwriter. My friend was waving her hands before I finished my sentence: "No, don't do that. Write songs. We need songs." On the plane ride home I took out my notebook and wrote, "It's too heavy to carry and impossible to leave." I went home and, over the next several months, wrote an entire record, *Tell Me What You Know*, about the young woman I had met. When I interviewed people at IJM and asked what they would want people to know about their experiences, one friend said, "While full healing can take many years, I'm always amazed that within minutes of freedom, there is humor, there are songs."

Tell me what you know
About God and the world and the human soul
How so much can go wrong
And still there are songs.[13]

The personally redemptive part of bearing witness to hard things and trying to tell the truth about them is that, in turn, this has rescued me. I had no idea how desperately I needed to move from a hereafter faith to an embodied gospel. In bearing witness to broken places in myself and in my community, I have seen the restorative and reconciling work of Jesus, and that testimony has revived me in these days of cynicism and anger.

Say It All: Keep It Human

Being generative does not preclude speaking to hard things or inviting good questions and debate, but it does include, as Mako states, a vision for "common flourishing." Nothing squelches honest thought and witness-bearing like forgetting another's humanity.

I was thinking recently about a scene in the movie *Wall-E*. The robot EVE has come to earth on a mission to find living organisms. She has a directive. Wall-E, an outdated model who has been all alone on earth for a long time, is eager to start a friendship. EVE and Wall-E are just beginning to warm to each other when her sensor is triggered by a living plant. She stiffens, becomes robotic, takes the plant into her storage compartment, and goes into hibernation—she is in Directive Mode. Wall-E does not understand what is happening. He puts an umbrella over her and strings up lights. He tries to hold her hand. He is giving care, doing human things, while she has become less human, closed off.

These days it's easy to replicate that process in our relationships; our conversations are fraught. So many topics can send us into Directive Mode, where we shut down and start robotically reciting the script for that directive. As a songwriter who is attempting to be generative, I have to fight to stay open and to resist dehumanizing rhetoric and propaganda.

I believe in the idea that we "vote" with our lives, money, and time. But if I feel as though my sole identity is as a walking representative of my church, my denomination, or my political party, then my speech and creativity are reduced to propaganda. I have to ask myself if I am stifling honest inquiry because I'm afraid to admit a flaw in the groups with which I most closely identify. I must consider whether I'm afraid that to speak honestly to issues within will be disloyal. If a pastor or a politician acts egregiously, there is a flurry of speech to defend and explain it away because of the damage it might do to the church or the party. I remember well how the denomination I grew up in weathered scandals with several notable personalities—I remember the secrecy, protection, and denial. I also remember the day I realized with relief, *I don't have to defend indefensible things*. My identity doesn't come from these organizations, and while the body of Christ is essential to my faith, I don't have to protect any particular organization at the expense of transparency and honest inquiry.

In this cultural moment when women are gaining courage to speak out about their experiences with abuse, and men are sharing their deepest moments of pain at the hands of an abuser, it is heart-breaking to hear many Christian leaders retreat, defend, explain away, or, even worse, respond with silence. God isn't silent about his heart for the vulnerable, and I want to be found standing with those who are seeking justice.

When the lights come up on this town
When the thing goes down
I want to be on the side of justice
When the lights come up on this town
When the thing goes down
I want to be on the side of mercy
When the lights come up
I want to be telling the truth.[14]

I was recently in a conversation with fellow Christians about what we think we have to offer the world. Some believed we are being attacked by the world for our faith and witness to the joy and generosity of Christ. Others argued that we are blind to our own subculture and all of its codes and privilege, that our testimony has lost all power because we elevate tribalism and nationalism. I sat there and thought, *I have seen both of these things*. I have seen the unparalleled generosity of God's people—and I testify! I have seen an incredible callousness toward the refugee in the name of Christian nationalism—and I cry out! I know devout people who spend their time and energy serving others because of their faith—and I testify! I have spoken with believers who think that current, structural racism is a figment of someone's imagination—and I cry out! Lord, have mercy!

I pray for courage to say what I'm seeing even if it is going against the grain of my group's directive and may cause me to lose favor or cost me financially. I pray for the wisdom to sense when I'm shutting down and entering Directive Mode, and I ask how to best fight the things that make me less human and make others less than human to me.

In the song "It's Me," I explore a moment of forgetting another's humanity in the context of my marriage. At the beginning of the song my husband, Troy, and I are in a great place and tenderness is the grace we are living in. But something hurtful is said, and—almost against both of our wishes—a coldness descends on us. We retreat deep inside ourselves and attempt a conversation, but all tenderness is gone.

> *Run for your life*
> *All tenderness is gone*
> *In the blink of an eye*
> *All good-will has withdrawn*
> *We mark out our paces and stare out from our faces*
> *But baby you and I are gone, gone, gone.*

I remember standing at my kitchen island thinking, *Where is the boy I love inside this man? Where is the girl inside me that loves that boy?* I remember wondering if we had any chance of connecting before our hurt and angry autopilot-selves made a complete mess of things.

> *Deep down inside the girl's waking up*
> *She's calling out to the boy she loves*
> *It's me.*[15]

If I can feel that detached from a person I live with and genuinely love, how much more am I capable of acting less than human with people I don't even know in real life? It is a divine gift to see the inherent value in each other. Sometimes I wonder if this isn't the whole

97

point of our faith, the whole work of Christ in our hearts. The Exodus story speaks of a plague of darkness so profound that "people could not see one another" (Ex. 10:23). I think we are fighting a similar darkness now, and we need divine help and wisdom to speak truth while pursuing each other's flourishing.

Say It All: A Safe Place to Say It All

In 2011, the question of what Troy and I would put into a bombed-out crater was answered with a place: Art House North. We had been all over the country and had put many songs into the world. We were longing for a place at home where we could share with our community some of the things we had experienced on the road.

The inspiration for Art House North came from Charlie Peacock and Andi Ashworth, who founded the first Art House in Nashville. Charlie and Andi created a place that awakened the kingdom imagination in people—a place of hospitality, generative life, creativity, conversation, and hope. Nashville had many outlets for artists to seek advice about their careers or how to approach their businesses, but Art House was the one place where they could talk meaningfully about their role in the world as artists and Christ-followers. It was fascinating to see how the work of Art House was simply the river that Charlie and Andi were moving along, but they opened it up and invited us and many others to join them. Sometimes we were making a record, sometimes we were gathered to learn about God's heart for justice, and sometimes we were simply having dinner with an eclectic array of guests.

Troy and I launched Art House North in the West End of St. Paul, Minnesota, in January 2011. We are one of three Art Houses around the country. Each reflects its distinctive community, but we share a tagline: "Creative Community for the Common Good." This is where we have attempted to move away from the culture wars and toward cultivating a garden. We have been surprised by neighborhood partnerships that have rooted Art House North in our community—a local church that meets on the weekend, a theater company that does three shows a year and hosts theater camps for kids, and a regular rabbinic Bible study for artists. A favorite new tradition is an annual square dance. There is nothing quite like blocking off the street for a few hours and inviting neighbors of all ages to dance. After last summer's dance my friend Mike said, "I can't think of another place where you see people smiling for two hours straight."

In addition to these regular rhythms, Troy and I host events and programs at Art House North. Like Charlie and Andi, we have attempted to root these activities in the flow of the river we are already moving along. Our kids are school age, so we started School of Rock–style music lessons for kids in the neighborhood called "Let's Rock," where kids could learn an instrument in a jam-band setting.

There is an intimacy to Art House North that lends itself to thoughtful conversations. Our building seats only 140 people, which wonderfully eliminates conversations about scaling and growth strategies. We often start planning an event by asking ourselves, what do we want to talk about? My favorite series we host is called "Artists Respond." This is where we call three to five artists with a topic and simply ask them to respond with their art. We don't tell them what to say or what conclusion to reach. We held the first Artists Respond the week after the shooting at Sandy Hook. The news cycle was already moving on, and I felt I had barely had space to grieve, even at church. I invited five artists to respond: a local poet, a cellist, a thespian, a songwriter, and a dancer. They did what no panel discussion or think piece could ever do. Our poet friend read a piece on the Cellist of Sarajevo, and the cellist played the famous Adagio from the same story. My theater friend, who was at the time in a one-woman play of *I Am Anne Frank*, performed a monologue from the play, "Who would ever think that so much went on in the soul of a little girl." My friend the dancer performed a stunning piece that started in slow mourning, *"Walk with me Lord, walk with me,"* and built until we were all on our feet. Finally, my songwriter friend closed with songs of truth-telling and lament. It was a sacred experience I won't forget. We had a safe place to be vulnerable, to bear witness together, and to say it all.

Our most recent Artists Respond was on Creation Care. The artists we invited to perform in turn invited all of us to reimagine our relationship with creation. It was a lovely night, full of inspiration. I walked home with a full heart, so grateful for a place where we could ask our questions and explore the breadth and depth of the reconciling work of God in Jesus. I was reminded of Paul's words in Colossians:

> For in him all the fullness of God was pleased to dwell, and through him God was pleased to reconcile to himself all things, whether on earth or in heaven, by making peace through the blood of his cross. (1:19–20)

As a songwriter, and now as one who facilitates the creative voices of others, I am called to walk without fear toward the bombed-out craters all around us, to bear witness to the whole spectrum of human experience, and to teach Ruby that even in these days we can say it all to a God who hears it all.

THE STORYTELLER

LECRAE

I AM A STORYTELLER, AND LIKE MOST GOOD STORYTELLERS, MY stories are complex, filled with complex people. There are seldom pure heroes or pure villains. In our lives, as in the Bible, our villains have surprising strengths and our heroes have tragic weaknesses, and there are lots of people in between. But this blurring of lines unsettles people.

As a public figure who blurs the lines between sacred and secular, I've grown accustomed to being misunderstood. I've gone in the same weekend from sharing stages with artists who write drug-induced tributes to hedonism to speaking at church conferences. We love to see things as black and white; complexity can be confusing. Instead of taking time to marvel at the differences and beauty of nuance, we'd often rather dismiss it and opt for the familiar.

I experienced the tyranny of the familiar during my first trip to Paris. I had always imagined Paris to be some kind of utopia, where everything would be beautiful, inviting, and easy. But I found being there very difficult. The language was different; the food was different; the culture was different. I thought I would love Paris, but these differences were initially a huge barrier to my enjoyment of the city. I found it difficult to do simple things like order a meal or have a conversation.

After two days I was exhausted and yearned for something familiar. Within a week I found myself opting for American fast-food chains over gourmet French meals simply because they were easy and familiar. Because I was so enamored at the thought of Paris, my romantic idealization created more problems for me than I thought. It's hard to have a romantic dinner with your wife when you're both struggling to understand the menu.

My preconceptions were challenged, and I didn't like it. It was easier to stick with what I knew. But many people I know who kept fighting through the unfamiliarity of differences discovered the beauty of diversity, language, and culture of Paris.

It sometimes takes work to fully see and appreciate something— especially if that something is outside our experience. Typically, the characters we see in society—from athletes to politicians to celebrities— aren't afforded the opportunity to be fully known and understood. Oftentimes we don't know their stories; we only know the narratives that have been attributed to them.

The way the story of rap music is distorted hits even closer to home for me. I have spent many hours working to convince Christians that rap music is valuable. Some Christians see it as a form of art used solely to glorify violence and misogyny. But although rap music is used in this way, those uses are not inherent to the art or its origins. Rap music is in many ways an articulation of a narrative that describes and explains the circumstances of a community. Rap music is descriptive, an account of a reality encountered by the artist. That accounting, a form of prophetic witness, has value. What's more, it shaped me as an artist. I wouldn't be here without the forerunners who created the rap music that many people dismiss as debased. Without all the gritty tales of the streets and the hedonistic celebration music that influenced me, I wouldn't know how to rap or speak the language of the culture.

Those who came before me taught me how to describe the reality that I encounter. They told stories. I tell stories. We all create narratives.

We tell stories to give meaning to otherwise messy situations and to reconcile in our minds what all the chaos means. We create heroes and villains to make sense of our stories. Who will be the hero, and who will be the villain? Americans are great at telling these kinds of stories. From the details surrounding the "discovery" of America, to the actual horrors behind our beloved Thanksgiving holiday, we omit historical facts for a more palatable sense of the past.

Sometimes our heroes are more villainous and our villains more heroic than we think. From the endorsement of slavery by the nation's founding fathers to our romanticization of murderous mobsters like Al Capone, Western culture finds itself changing narratives for the sake of pride or prostituting tales of misogyny and violence for the sake of entertainment.

As a black man influenced by many of the aspects of urban culture, I didn't become a responsible father and role model simply because I snapped out of it. Instead, I was influenced by people who didn't write me off as a villain but saw me as a would-be hero in the making.

Neither we nor our heroes are as flawless as we would like to think. Nor are the villains we deplore always that much different from us, were we faced with their same life circumstances. There is always a story behind the characters, one that can reveal these nuances. It takes humility to listen with empathy to the stories of the people we encounter.

Part of that listening involves understanding worldviews. A worldview is a deep-seated, often subconscious, way of seeing the world. Only after listening empathetically and trying to understand others' worldviews can we learn how to build authentic relationships across ethnic, cultural, and religious divides. I'm not speaking simply of working relationships but of true friendships.

We can realize that the stories we hear, and the stories we share, are not simply about facts and propositions. Sharing stories means sharing emotions and rendering ourselves vulnerable to others. And we can recognize the full range of emotions in our stories. Anger can be good if it is constructive and not destructive. Constructive anger leads to passionately fighting for the rights of the marginalized; destructive anger leads to burning buildings and rioting.

Over the last few years, I've worked to challenge people about the difference between constructive and destructive anger. From TedX talks to editorials to songs, I have pleaded with others to understand the emotion of anger in a more nuanced way. Of course, there are still misunderstandings, and I've had to learn to be patient and persistent. People will always gravitate toward a story that aligns with their current way of seeing the world. It's our default setting. An example from my own life might help explain.

I've been pepper sprayed on three different occasions. Pepper spray burns. It burns bad. Your throat closes up. Your eyes swell as if someone has doused them with gallons of habanero juice. These experiences were so traumatizing I still vividly remember each one. I would need additional chapters to begin to tell those stories.

I wonder what thoughts you've started to have about my encounters with pepper spray as you read the last paragraph. Was I the villain, provoking someone to respond in self-defense? Or was I the hero, stepping in to save the day and sprayed inadvertently? Or maybe I was both? We must have a storyline for those things because without a storyline we struggle to attach meaning to the incident. We desperately desire things to make sense. We labor over scientific theories, historical narratives, astrology, and religions to give meaning to what happens around us. We are hardwired to want to know *why*.

That's why we are drawn to stories. Stories help us develop meaning. Even if we get the story wrong, we have closure on the *why*.

The way we see the world is shaped through a story. Our meaning comes from some sort of master narrative. People connect with and prefer stories over charts and graphs—ask any teacher or preacher. Like many, I almost always find myself checking out of lectures and sermons and daydreaming until a story is being told. It's almost magical.

We spend billions of dollars each year watching stories in movie theaters and on televisions and computers. We look for relatable archetypes and characters with which we identify or heroes we admire. And so we struggle to attach meaning to things *without* a storyline. As a result, what most of us do to find meaning in our broken world is separate that world into good guys and bad guys.

Every story has essentials. Something turns the world upside down. Something is broken. A hero exists to set it straight and repair what is broken. And a villain appears who is an adversary or enemy.

The incidents in Ferguson, Missouri, following the 2014 killing of Michael Brown provide an example. What happened there means something. But what it means depends on the story being told.

One narrative insists that the black community consists of good people with bad circumstances. The local police are bad people who abuse power. The black community must fight to show that black lives matter in this country and bring police to task. That gives many people meaning to what transpired in this St. Louis suburb.

Another narrative is that the police are the heroes doing the best they can in a dangerous profession. People like Mike Brown are the villains who break the law and face the unfortunate consequences of their actions. We can't allow race to blind us from seeing that crime is crime and the justice system will ultimately work to show what really happened.

Both of the aforementioned examples have different protagonists and antagonists. Different good guys and bad guys. It's as if no one can see the events transpiring in Missouri without a narrative that allows it to make sense. What's more, we have trouble digesting a narrative that doesn't fit our worldview. It's actually easier for us to believe a false narrative that fits our outlook on the world than a true narrative that shakes and shatters our perspective. And that is true regardless of where we stand.

However, a Christian worldview, marked by the biblical storyline, stands apart from ordinary, conventional storylines. It shows that in the grand scheme, we are all guilty. We are all villains, the bad guys. The true evil is sin showing its face through broken humanity, and it touches every one of us. The one true hero is Jesus and his power to restore broken hearts and repair the infrastructures corrupted by sin.

I remember as a kid hearing the story of David and Goliath. Goliath was a menacing, nine-foot-tall Philistine warrior evoking fear in Israel's army. More than likely, the Philistines were more advanced in warfare and had great advantages in weaponry over Israel. So no brave soul in Israel's army was willing to match Goliath head-to-head for the sake of the nation. Then along came a small, young shepherd boy named David. With great courage and dependence on God, David defeated Goliath with a slingshot, and Israel was victorious.

If you are like me, you understood the meaning of this story to be something along the lines of "trust God even if you're the underdog and ill-equipped and you, too, can be a hero like David." Though I believe there is truth to that view, I believe more that God is communicating through this story his master narrative. We are all Israel, cowering and scared. Goliath represents the powers of darkness and evil that are clearly having their way with us. We stand powerless, but God sends a Savior. An unassuming hero who doesn't fight in the traditional ways. Instead, his valiant and vigilant dependency on the Father brings an end to darkness and liberates the people.

Sin is the antagonist and Jesus is the protagonist. Like any good villain, sin and Satan will actively recruit us to the dark side—inviting us to abuse power, to riot, to kill, to hate.

But Christ invites us to come into the glorious light. The true hero shows us how to love, empathize, forgive, and work to restore what sin has broken.

~

The beauty and wonder of art is its ability to tell stories. The artist is a storyteller—as is the painter, the filmmaker, the songwriter. By using stories, artists push people toward the master narrative of our creation, our fall, our redemption, and our journey through the wilderness with God. People are drawn to story. The Lord of the Rings saga are some of my favorite films, second only to John Singleton's *Boyz n the Hood*. They show us human depravity, the darkness of the heart, and our lives wrestling with a sin nature.

In *The Lion, the Witch, and the Wardrobe*, C. S. Lewis reveals God's master narrative. A great and perfect king gave himself up for an utterly undeserving, conniving boy. The world is drawn to the story, not to a bunch of facts laid out about sacrificial love. You can't grasp the meaning of the facts without the story being told.

The artist can either use story to help people see God's master narrative or point to a lesser, unworthy protagonist. Years ago, I wrote a song called "Welcome to America," which told three different stories from three perspectives of America.

The first verse is from the vantage point of a young person in the inner city who sees himself as the protagonist in a struggle against systemic oppression. He believes that effort will somehow make him stronger and bring him to a better place. Criminal enterprise isn't his preference, but in a jobless community with subpar educational facilities, it's the best hand he's been dealt. This young person plans to engage in such criminal activity in hopes of relieving his family of poverty. America is the antagonist. The country's biased systems don't take into consideration the overwhelming circumstances of generational poverty and miseducation that existed well before any crime was committed. America made him this way. America is the source of all the pain and brokenness.

The second verse is the narrative of a soldier who has struggled and fought for the country he loves. His antagonist is an unpatriotic tribe of Americans who don't appreciate what he's done for them. He's lost everything for their gain. He has lost his marriage, his mental health, the love of his friends, and nearly his own life. He believes in this country and believes that, though it is not perfect, America and its founding principles are pure. Believing in these principles encourages him to believe his fighting was not in vain. Still, he's realizing that the people and country he fights for do not share the same patriotism.

The final verse is the story of an immigrant who can't understand why Americans are so ungrateful for the wonderful country they have. From his perspective, Americans are blessed with bountiful freedom and opportunity. People in this country have an abundance of food and education. Clean water, beds, and health care are also provided. The immigrant speaks of working in sweatshops to provide Americans their luxuries. Without complaint, this foreigner just wants to join our ranks. America is the hero. This country offers the freedom he longs for. Yet once this person arrives, the immigration laws keep him from obtaining a green card.

The irony is these stories are all true. They just aren't comprehensively true. Each story attributes every ounce of the evil to the villain and places ultimate hope in the wrong hero.

Christians, of all people, should recognize that America is not the ultimate source of brokenness nor the ultimate source of joy. America is not the ultimate hero. The problem (the villain) is always sin, and the solution (the hero) is always the gospel. Of course, that's a simplification of how sin and depravity have not only tainted the hearts of people but also tainted our hands and the things we build with them. Sinful people have created institutions and infrastructures that are negatively affecting the world today. Laws, businesses, and common practices created by depraved hearts and hands hundreds of years ago are still producing bad fruit. It will take redeemed people to restore these broken systems.

It's often hard to see our role in this grand story. Who exactly are we to stand up to such great adversity? Yet here is how in many ways the narrative of Jesus jumps out at me. I relate to his humanity—more specifically to the simplicity and frailty of his humanity. My own story follows a path that I sometimes read in parallel to his story—though I am neither a hero nor a villain. Or maybe I am a little of both.

I was born to a single mother, who initially survived only with government assistance, and to a father who struggled with addiction. My mother received no visitations from angels prior to my birth—at least none that she's told me about. In kindergarten, I set off firecrackers in the school bathroom. In first grade, I got into a fight with John Carney and knocked out his front tooth. The tooth was already loose, but the other kids didn't know that. I didn't run from Herod and move to Egypt in fear for my life as a young boy as Jesus did. I also didn't impress the local Bible scholars as a child.

By middle school, I was busy being suspended for inciting gang violence and being escorted home by police for petty crimes. This pattern (which continued well into my late teen years) was the type of pattern that makes society say, "He's probably not going to amount to much." Despite these setbacks—some of my own doing and some done to me—I was not alone.

This is the background that enables me to relate to Jesus' story. Society didn't think much of him or his kingdom while he was here in human form. In Matthew 13:31–32, he said, "The kingdom of heaven is like a mustard seed that someone took and sowed in his field; it is the smallest of all the seeds, but when it has grown it is the greatest of shrubs and becomes a tree, so that the birds of the air come and make nests in its branches."

In our technological society and culture, all this plant talk doesn't translate as easily. Jesus, however, was speaking to a very agricultural world. Plants, farms, and animals were commonplace. His audience would have understood the elements in this parable. They would have known that, eventually, the mustard seed grows to a size that you can't miss. Jesus was saying that people often don't think much of the beginning of something that is ultimately going to become great. The kingdom of God is impressive. The origins of a mustard seed are far from impressive. But God's kingdom, like the mustard seed, shouldn't be measured by its seemingly insignificant beginnings.

Small things that seem insignificant but later become something greater: I understand this concept all too well. After I nearly failed the ninth grade, my high school guidance counselor told my mother that I should be in classes for people with learning disabilities. I was told I shouldn't be in the general population with my peers but should instead be enrolled in an alternative school. I was counted out early on. Jesus also knows this narrative well. He started out with twelve ordinary men with seemingly insignificant beginnings who ended up changing the world.

He lived and died in what was considered a little ghetto town of the Roman Empire. He is mentioned only in passing by the leading historical sources of his time. But today his name and power have spread throughout the world.

The story of seemingly vulnerable people doing amazing things is one we understand. It's something we see all around us. These are people we know and admire. Some of our cultural pioneers are ambassadors who were also counted out.

Walt Disney was fired from the *Kansas City Star* in 1919 because his editor said he "lacked imagination and had no good ideas."[1] Oprah Winfrey was born in a small town whose name I can't even pronounce. She was told she wouldn't make it as a news reporter because she couldn't separate her emotions from her stories.[2] Most of my favorite rap icons, from Jay-Z to Tupac, have background stories of being in the lowest of circumstances and being overlooked only to emerge as cultural influencers.

My favorite picture of the proverbial mustard seed comes in the form of a movie, *The Matrix*. This is one of my all-time favorite movies. I never understood the depth of my connections to this film until years after I first watched it. I love sci-fi and action/adventure films, but most of all I love a good story. The film focuses on an average and "invisible" tech worker by day named Thomas Anderson—but by night he's a relentless computer hacker under the handle of Neo. As a kid, I thought I had figured out life's deeper meanings when I discovered the letters *Neo* could be rearranged to spell "one." (Urban nerd alert.)

Even though Neo is unassuming, an infamous leader named Morpheus sees more in him. Morpheus has been given a prophecy that Neo will be the leader of a newly liberated world. It's not that Morpheus has faith in Neo; as a matter of fact, there are times he doubts this young man's potential. But he has faith in a greater substance: a prophecy. Another character, Trinity, also believes Neo is the chosen one, though to her he seems slow to learn and full of fear. In faith, they invest in Neo, offering him their time, talents, and treasures, and they find that not only is he a leader, but he is a leader like none other.

Narratives like this remind us that God knows we are quick to dismiss the potential of what appears small to us. At the same time, we are all frail, broken, and imperfect people. Yet we are people whom God is pleased to embrace and adopt, thereby bringing us into the greatness we were created for. Many of us fight to find purpose and greatness outside of God, but it is only through him that we find it.

Why did Jesus exercise more faith and investment in those coming from humble beginnings? Those twelve men had already failed in many ways. Society had already told them, "You're not good enough." But God knew they were good enough—and he says *you* are more than enough. God says, *I know from the outside you look like a little mustard seed, but I wish you could see the tree you're going to become.*

Likewise, society said to little Lecrae—who came from a backwater town and a single-parent, drug-afflicted home and was in and out of trouble—that he wasn't ever going to amount to much of anything. But those who believed in me continued to invest in me. God was guiding things for my benefit and his glory the whole time. No one anticipated that I would attend college, pursue entrepreneurship, and craft art that would travel the world and inspire people. I'm all the evidence you need to know that mustard seeds do grow.

I tell stories because I have a voice and an audience who respects my voice. I tell them as accurately as I can and as passionately as possible. The fact that many of the world's stories are left out and untold motivates me. I know that often whoever holds the pen gets to write the story. Many people have never been given a voice, let alone a pen, to begin to tell their stories. In fact, people have been convinced certain stories and history don't matter. We often hear of the French Revolution and the Renaissance era, but what of the art and history of Dominica? We know Philip articulated the gospel of Jesus to a man from Ethiopia, but do we know the church history of Ethiopia? If we aren't careful we will believe these are stories that do not need to be heard simply because they aren't being told.

I've spent quite a bit of time in eastern Africa. I've learned to listen. I've learned to soak in the culture and history of the people there. I've come not only to serve but also to learn. The people in the Kole district of Uganda have a story that I believe my listeners should hear. Their stories of pain, suffering, resilience, and rebuilding have inspired me. They are a people with myriad resources at their fingertips. Unfortunately, having their country historically cut off from trade and opportunity left them cut off from both sharing in the innovation of foreigners and offering their brilliance to us. I've offered my time and talents to their cause, and I have been to their villages and learned their stories and benefited as well.

Michael, a resident of the Kole district, is a man roughly fifty years old. He was formerly a bricklayer in the village. It was grueling work that injured his back. He was trusting God to help him pay for his grandchildren to attend college. He wanted better for them. God answered. Due to the partnership of a foreign agency, he was made aware of how fertile his land was. He learned to plant trees and now has a plantation of fruit trees as well as other plants he's turned into an enterprise. His grandchildren's education is secure. His story inspires us because in many ways it's our story. Many of us have faced insurmountable odds and are antagonized by things like fear or abject poverty. Still, we trust in a divine hero to bring us through. The beauty of having a divine hero is that we are never left in despair. God never fails. Fear believes God will get it wrong; bitterness believes he did. Yet, though we've all experienced those feelings, hopefully we still trust in his divine plan. Sometimes part of that plan is revealed to us, but even more will not be revealed until we see his glory in full.

God did not save us through a bunch of principles and science. He did not speak to us through graphs and charts. He did not inspire us to use oblique statistical references to change systems and infrastructures that are historically tainted with sin and evil. Instead, he gave us a story. A story of creation, fall, redemption, and consummation. A story of a man named Jesus. And through that story he asks us to follow him with our lives and with stories of our own.

THE TRANSLATOR

JOHN INAZU

MY DAY JOB FOR MOST OF MY ADULT LIFE HAS FORCED ME TO
be a translator. As a lawyer, and now as a teacher, I have had to make
words and ideas accessible to audiences unfamiliar with them. That
challenge is not unique to me—it is true of many professions. It is also
true for every one of us in our personal relationships across difference:
each of us is called to the task of translation. And in this personal
translation through our lives, we have a God-given opportunity. We
are, as Paul wrote, "ambassadors for Christ, since God is making his
appeal through us" (2 Cor. 5:20).

We can think of translating in the most general sense as making the unknown known, making the inaccessible more accessible.
Sometimes we translate by using familiar concepts to explain unfamiliar ones or by building from simple points of connection to more
complex ones. Many of us experience this process when we learn a
new language. When I was in high school, I began to learn Spanish
by seeing unfamiliar words placed alongside familiar ones. I learned
that *abuela* meant "grandmother" and *gato* meant "cat." At some point
I moved on to grammar, which meant understanding how those words
fit together within a broader framework: *mi abuela le gusta mi gato*

("My grandmother likes my cat"). And I eventually discovered exceptions to the rules. The exceptions were easier to learn in Spanish than in English, with its dizzying number of obscure departures from the basic rules, like "*i* before *e* except after *c* or when sounding like *a* as in *neighbor* or *weigh*."

The example of learning a new language illustrates the challenge of translation: we start with basic concepts, then we locate those concepts in broader frameworks, and finally, we discover that the frameworks don't always hold together as easily as we thought. All of this takes a great deal of practice. And often our need to practice never goes away. When I stopped learning Spanish in school, I soon lost even my basic ability to translate. Today, I remember only a few Spanish words and almost nothing of the broader frameworks; I had to google that sentence about my grandmother and cats.

Effective translation requires understanding the object of translation. When I was practicing law, I sometimes worked with engineers who were asked to testify in court. These men and women were some of the smartest people in the world—some of them were literally rocket scientists; others had invented path-breaking technology like the microchips in our cell phones. But I soon learned that engineers are not always very good translators. They know why something works and why it matters, but they do not always know how to explain it to others.

My job as a lawyer was to find words, metaphors, and analogies that would explain the technical expertise of engineers to nonspecialists who would decide the outcomes of high-stakes cases. And in order to do my job, I had to understand their expertise. I needed to understand before I could translate. That meant asking naive questions to my engineer witnesses and begging for their patience as I worked to wrap my head around ideas and concepts that were intuitive to them but opaque to me.

Today, as a law school teacher, I still need to know the object of translation. Like my high school Spanish teacher, I must be "fluent" in the subjects I teach. New cases and new issues arise, but part of the reason I can teach law is that I have come to understand a small part of the world at a fairly deep level. Of course, this wasn't always the case, and it is not always true of every course I teach. During my first year of teaching, I misread one of the cases in my criminal law class and thought it stood for exactly the opposite of what it said. This was the law school equivalent of explaining multiplication when you think you are explaining division. And because I had built my entire lesson plan around my misreading of the case, the more I tried to explain my incorrect understanding, the more confused the class became.

I no longer get cases backward in the subjects I teach—at least not as backward as I did in that first year of teaching. But subject-matter familiarity is only part of effective translation; I also have to know my audience. If I fail to understand my audience, I will not be an effective translator. As a teacher, part of knowing my audience means recognizing, as Ken Bain has written, that I "always have something new to learn—not so much about teaching techniques but about these particular students at this particular time and their particular sets of aspirations, confusions, misconceptions, and ignorance."[1] In other words, the experience of teaching is always new because the students are always different. Each class is a unique blend of experiences, personalities, and background understanding. And effective teaching—effective translation—depends upon my recognizing and understanding each of the unique dimensions of each new class of students.

Sometimes our audience brings not just unfamiliarity but also misinformation. It is hard enough translating to people who don't understand the object of translation. It is sometimes even harder when they think they already know what you are trying to explain to them.

That is particularly true when a presumed understanding is easier, simpler, or just more palatable than a correct one. Some of my law students are disappointed to learn how the law differs from what they have gleaned from movies and shows. Others are unsettled when they realize that the answer to many legal questions is not "yes" or "no" but "it depends."

Understanding the object of translation and the audience to whom I am translating still takes effort in my teaching. But like many people, I find it even more difficult—mentally, emotionally, and relationally—to translate my fundamental beliefs and convictions. Most of us confront this challenge at some point in our lives. We find ourselves in multiple worlds, having to bridge the differences between them.

I think of this as *the vocation of translation*. Like more ordinary examples of translation, the vocation of translation for Christians today requires knowing what we are translating and the audience to whom we are translating. Knowing what we are translating means knowing ourselves as we have been remade by our faith. We cannot share our core convictions and ourselves with others if we don't know how the gospel has shaped us. Loving our neighbor as ourselves, which Jesus commands us to do (Mark 12:31), will be disastrous if we don't know ourselves first as beloved by God.

The vocation of translating our lives adds another dimension to more ordinary forms of translation: personal risk. As a lawyer or a teacher, I bear some risk to my professional reputation if I translate ineffectively, like I did when I misread that case during my first year of teaching. But when I am translating *me*, the risk is far more personal. When I fail to explain *me* to an unfamiliar audience—whether to a large group or to a single individual—that failure can feel like personal rejection. Each of us risks this rejection every time we engage in the vocation of translation, every time we try to make ourselves—and the beliefs that animate us—known to others. As the theologian Lesslie Newbigin has observed: "Personal knowledge is impossible without risk; it cannot begin without an act of trust, and trust can be betrayed."[2]

In my life, the vocation of translation means living part of my life in the university and part of my life in the church. My university life includes teaching law students and undergraduates, writing scholarly articles that few people read, and spending long hours in faculty meetings, university committees, and obscure professional organizations. My church life includes worshiping and engaging with my local church, writing and speaking to Christian audiences, and investing my time and resources in local, national, and global ministries.

My vocation of translation means translating the university to some of my church friends and translating the church to some of my university friends. Living between these two worlds makes me a kind of bilingual translator—speaking the languages of two different cultures. Knowing both cultures well also means that I am not entirely at home in either one. On any given Wednesday, I might find myself in a faculty meeting with colleagues who simultaneously inspire and perplex me, thinking to myself, *These are not my people*. A few hours later, I am in church, with people who simultaneously inspire and perplex me, thinking to myself, *These are not my people*. Many of the people in one of these worlds know little about the people in the other. And in both worlds, otherwise thoughtful people sometimes substitute stereotypes and assumptions for personal knowledge and relationships. My afternoon faculty meeting and my evening church dinner occur within two miles of each other, but their relational distance feels much greater.

I used to think of translating between these two cultures as having "one foot in one world and one foot in the other." As a Christian professor at a non-Christian university, I saw myself as having one foot in the university and one foot in the church. But I came to see this metaphor as insufficient: being an effective translator often requires simultaneous immersion into two different contexts. In my case, it means having two feet in the university and two feet in the church.[3]

The analogy of two-footed immersion hits even closer to home when it comes to the challenge of translating between "white" and "nonwhite" worlds. As someone who is half-Japanese, I am both an "insider" and an "outsider" to white culture. That is partly a function of my physical appearance and partly a function of my lived experience. I feel it most acutely at the intersection of race and faith—where I find myself translating between the worlds inside and outside of "white evangelicalism."

I grew up in mostly white churches. I moved around a lot and found myself in many different church communities around the country—churches in Maryland, Kansas, California, Washington, Hawaii, New York, Colorado, North Carolina, Virginia, and South Dakota. My church communities were Episcopalian, Presbyterian, Methodist, Baptist, Evangelical Free, and nondenominational. But they were all mostly white—not only in their people but also in their culture. I was formed by practices and liturgies that reflected a certain kind of scriptural focus, worship style, rhythm, structure, tone, lament, and prayer. I was formed in churches that focused on certain issues and neglected others. Even our Christology reflected our whiteness: we saw Jesus, in Lecrae's memorable phrase, as "the European with the ultra perm and them soft eyes and them thin lips."[4] None of this made us self-consciously white—nobody ever called the pastor the "white pastor" or the musician the "white musician." And because this was the only church culture I knew, I never thought of it as "the white church." It was just "church."

But the fact that I came to see my church as just "church" is part of the point. This hit home for me when I gave a talk a few years ago to the Christian fellowship group at my alma mater. When I was in college the group was mostly white, with a few Asian students. When I returned for my talk twenty years later, the group was mostly Asian, with a few white students. The group to which I had returned felt to me like the "Asian Christian group." The music, humor, people, and style all felt Asian. But why? When the group had been mostly white during my time, it hadn't felt like the "white Christian group." I simply thought of it as "the Christian group," because I had acclimated myself to a white baseline for what felt normal. For similar reasons, the group twenty years later felt Asian instead of normal.

And yet I don't always see "white" as "normal." A recent example began with an exchange I had on social media with a prominent evangelical. This person had publicly endorsed the view that the Bible supported President Trump's proposal to build a wall between the United States and Mexico. I thought his appeal to Scripture was deeply flawed and suggested as much in my response to him: "I wonder at what point in the United States' genocidal westward expansion you would argue a wall would have been biblically justified." My point was that this country had long engaged in deeply un-Christian actions in its efforts to expand and mark its territory, and that those actions complicated efforts to claim biblical authority for protecting our borders. A few hours later, the prominent evangelical responded with a question for me: "When did you arrive?"

I was stunned by the response. I had to read it several times to make sure I was seeing it correctly. In that moment, I was the outsider, named as such through a racially insensitive comment by someone embedded in the white evangelical world. The fact that our exchange had begun over immigration policy made the comment sting all the more. In my case, my Japanese grandparents had been born in the United States—it was my great-grandparents who had "arrived" in this country. But my grandparents and my father had then been imprisoned at Manzanar during the Second World War, a part of my own story that made the outsider characterization particularly biting.

I do not mean to suggest that one must be nonwhite to understand why the comment "When did you arrive?" was so inappropriate. Plenty of white commentators weighed in to critique it. They, like me, could translate to the nonwhite evangelical world. But it was much harder for me to translate in the other direction, to understand the white evangelical world from which the comment was made and, ultimately, defended. In subsequent comments, my evangelical interlocutor called me "thin-skinned" and expressed "shock" that anyone would see his initial response as racist—he had, after all, "written two books about actual racism."

I wondered about the practices and influences that had shaped this person to think of his initial comment to me, to post it on social media, and to fail to grasp that it would be seen as racially insensitive. And it wasn't only his comment to me. It was also the argument that preceded it, which claimed a scriptural justification for the United States to build a wall along its Mexican border. More broadly, it is the unwavering support of many white evangelicals for a president whose politics and policies comfort some of them but whose words and actions mock Christian values and alienate nonwhite voices. Or the insistence of many white evangelicals that the United States is a "Christian nation," that something of "ours" has been lost to a more pluralistic and less accommodating culture. These perspectives in many ways reflect the white evangelical world from which I came. And it is a world that feels increasingly inaccessible to me.

There are ways in which I am tempted to wear my lack of empathy with the white evangelical world as a badge of honor. I often see myself in greater solidarity with my nonwhite brothers and sisters than I once did. I have become more aware of the immense challenges that nonwhite Christians confront when they work in predominantly white Christian institutions. I see arguments and issues that I did not previously understand. These are good things. But my difficulty understanding the white evangelical world is not itself good; it is a limitation on my ability to be an effective translator about things that matter to me. If I want to explain why some perspectives are misguided—if I want to show why I am not simply "thin-skinned"—I am going to need to keep working at translating effectively. That means I will have to engage with greater empathy. I will have to work to imagine two feet in the world of white evangelicalism even as I simultaneously stand with two feet outside of it. I will need to set aside words and emotions that instinctively come to mind. That is the task of the translator.

The limits of my empathy also point to the limits of my metaphor of having two feet firmly planted in two different contexts. Few of us who are called to be translators will find ourselves so fully immersed in multiple contexts that we are able to identify with each completely. In fact, part of being a translator means living with the inevitable tension of not being fully at home in any one place. The tension-inducing difference reflects the fracture of our world and the need for translators in the first place. We anticipate a world to come in which we will see fully even as we are fully known, but until then, we remain in a world of translators who see "in a mirror, dimly" (1 Cor. 13:12).

The vocation of translation means seeking understanding, even for the people and contexts that most escape our empathy. In the case of my dissonance with the world of white evangelicalism, part of seeking understanding means reminding myself that some arguments will not be won through sound bites on social media. Some arguments will take months and years of listening and explaining. My friend Rich McClure often reminds me of these challenges. Rich is the former CEO of United Van Lines, and he would be the first to admit that he comes out of the white evangelical world. But in 2016, Rich was appointed by our state's governor to co-chair the Ferguson Commission, which was tasked to assess the causes and aftermath of the events in Ferguson, Missouri, following the shooting of Michael Brown. Working closely with a black pastor (his commission co-chair) and other members of the African American community, Rich learned a language and a mind-set that was previously unknown to him. It was, by his own account, a slow and often painful process. And though he now spends much of his time translating these ideas back to the world of white evangelicalism, he often reminds me that this particular work of translation is never easy and often unsuccessful.

I suppose my own role as a translator between two worlds— between university and church, and between white and nonwhite worlds—helps explain my focus on humility, patience, and tolerance in my book *Confident Pluralism*. I see these characteristics as critical not only to living with difference but also to the act of translating across difference.

Humility acknowledges that I cannot always prove to others why I believe that I am right and they are wrong. Many of us are shaped over time by the habits, practices, and institutions in which we are embedded. We come to see the world through those lenses, and as my friend Rich reminds me, challenging a way of seeing is not as easy as deconstructing a logical fallacy or pointing out a knowledge gap. Change, if it comes, often depends on relationships of trust that are built over time. Sometimes the relationships that lead to change will take a lifetime.

Patience means restraining myself when people in either of my worlds project onto me their assumptions about "that other world." Sometimes the inapt characterizations bother me, but more often they amuse me, like the time a faculty colleague said to me, "I don't get you;

you're religious, but you care about poor people." Or the many times I've heard from Christians who tell me they can't trust a "liberal law professor" like me. I regularly encounter people in my university world who assume from my faith that I am a Republican who likes guns. People in my church world often assume from my profession that I am a Democrat who reads only the *New York Times*. (For the record, I have been politically independent my entire life, I have disliked guns since losing three high school classmates to gun violence, and I am deeply ambivalent about the *New York Times*.)

Tolerance means a willingness to distinguish between people and their ideas. In my two worlds, I encounter people whose ideas give me pause. Not everybody, to be sure. Like most people, I have friends whose beliefs and ideas are closer to my own. But many of my acquaintances—and some of my friends—require me to move tolerance from an idea to a practice. Both the university colleague whose understanding of diversity so clearly excludes religious diversity and the church parishioner who lacks any understanding of diversity at all hold beliefs I find harmful to our society. But tolerance means remembering that both are human beings who are more complex than the stereotypes I might ascribe to them, and that I likely have something to learn from each of them.

Most of us could stand to be more humble, patient, and tolerant with each other. This is not to say that our differences are unimportant. Many of our differences matter a great deal, and to suggest otherwise is ultimately a form of relativism. But we can still choose to be gracious across our differences. We can also avoid demonizing others, which might help us better understand their perspectives. Good lawyers know that the success of their own arguments depends upon knowing the best arguments of the other side. The best arguments are not caricatures; they represent the most charitable and most sophisticated accounts of an opposing view. When we demonize the other side, we miss important insights that can only be learned through charitably understanding a different perspective. We lose the possibility of finding common ground.

For most of us, finding common ground will mean partnering with people, institutions, and movements that diverge in important respects from our core convictions. We seek common ground with people who hold views antithetical to the gospel whenever we work with, support, or vote for Republicans or Democrats. We facilitate religious beliefs and practices that we believe are wrong when we rightly advocate for the religious liberty of all. Most of us work for institutions that engage in some forms of injustice alongside their good endeavors. Living in the world means seeking common ground with people and pursuits that are not gospel-centered.

Seeking common ground across difference not only advances common interests but also bridges relational distance. I think of my friend Eboo Patel, one of the national leaders of interfaith work on college and university campuses and the founder of an important organization called the Interfaith Youth Core. Eboo's blend of Muslim faith and progressive politics lead us to differ over many important issues. But we have found ways to partner in our advocacy for humility, patience, and tolerance across these differences, even though doing so increases the space for each of us to advance views with which the other disagrees.[5]

Eboo and I speak, teach, and write together. And we have become friends. We talk about each other's backgrounds, families, and dreams. We argue about theories of change and undergraduate readings. We laugh at each other's jokes—at least the first time we hear them; we have now spoken together enough times that we can finish them for each other. And we mourn together. After my father learned of his cancer diagnosis, Eboo checked in regularly with phone calls and texts. And when my father died, Eboo was one of the first people to reach out to me. Eboo's prayers are quite different from mine, but I am grateful when he prays for me.

In *Confident Pluralism*, I suggest that we can find common ground with others even when we lack a shared understanding of the common good. But this will most likely happen through interpersonal relationships. I am increasingly convinced that most of us need to start locally, or at least with relationships, like mine with Eboo, that bring us into regular contact with one another. These relationships will require a kind of vulnerability as we engage in the vocation of translation. They will mean sharing parts of ourselves and taking personal risks: we are translating not only words but our lives. And for Christians, the aspirations of humility, patience, and tolerance—and the virtues of faith, hope, and love—will help us in the work of translation to which we are called.

PART THREE

EMBODYING OUR ENGAGEMENT

THE BRIDGE BUILDER

SHIRLEY V. HOOGSTRA

MY MOTHER MODELED BRIDGE BUILDING FOR ME. ONCE, WHEN
I was a child, she and I were in a rest-stop washroom, the kind of place
where people typically keep their eyes down. As I washed my hands,
I heard a thud. I turned around and saw my mother rush into a stall
to help a disabled woman who had fallen. Though my mother did not
know her, she entered into an uncomfortable space without blinking
an eye to help a woman who was exposed, frightened, and helpless.
My mother's simple act gave me a concrete example of how to move
toward my neighbor with love, respect, and humility.

I do not always follow her example. Too often, I respond out of
fear rather than generosity. In 2016, ISIS-connected terrorists killed
dozens and wounded hundreds in three bombings in Belgium. The
attacks unfolded against a backdrop of a massive influx of immigrants
pouring into Europe from war-torn countries. These immigrants faced
freezing weather and perilous seas, arriving from the Middle East and
Africa. Images circulating in media outlets were stunning, as men,
women, and children in life jackets tumbled out of rafts, many barely
alive, some already dead. One photograph captured the human dimension of the journey more than any other: a dead child's body washed

up on shore. Yet after the Brussels bombings, these immigrants—
many of whom were Muslim—were suddenly viewed as dangerous,
suspect, and unwelcome.

I was slated to travel to Europe with my family six weeks after the
bombings, a trip that would take us to the very site of the carnage. I
changed our travel plans.

Pope Francis took a different approach, one closer to the spirit my
mother showed to me. He moved toward the immigrants. Two days
after the bombings, Pope Francis washed and kissed the feet of twelve
migrants from Somalia, Eritrea, Syria, and Pakistan—the very people
I was afraid of. He said, "We, Muslims, Hindus, Catholics, Copts,
Evangelicals, have different cultures and religions, but we are brothers
and we want to live in peace."[1] The pope's actions and statements
were in contrast to those of many in Europe and the United States.
His message of mercy restored dignity. He modeled courage, love, and
respect for the displaced, the poor, and the vulnerable. He bridged a
chasm and acted out of the belief that human beings are image bearers
of God, and he, as a servant of God, was a servant to them.

It was in watching the pope's selfless extension of mercy and
thinking back to my mother's example that I realized I want my life
to reflect that kind of bridge building.

The Structure of Bridges

Building relational bridges is much like building physical ones: it
requires innovation, investment, and an eye toward structures that
will withstand the test of time. And like a physical bridge, a relational
bridge requires a strong anchor in two different places: one's own faith
and values, and one's neighbor's best interests. Bridge building means

cultivating a mind-set that allows us to absorb cognitive dissonance, span paradox, and balance competing interests or complexity for the well-being of ourselves and others. I believe there are four qualities essential to relational bridge building: respect, humility, trustworthiness, and love.

Respect

Bridge building is not possible if you do not have a genuine interest in knowing and understanding the person on the other side of the chasm you seek to traverse. And this interest must culminate in respect. Respect stems from the belief that people bear the image of God. It allows for a high view of every human person, regardless of their past, present, or future personal relationship with Jesus. Respect isn't a synonym for agreement, but it does impact the way a person disagrees. One cannot respect another and harbor a desire to overpower that person through insults, dismissal, or derogatory actions.

Humility

A bridge builder strives to be a learner, which requires a posture of openness: "What don't I know; what could I learn?" As I approach someone or some problem, I remember that I will not know everything at first glance and there is more I will know in the future. First impressions may be true but are almost always incomplete. A generous spirit values wanting to know and understand another point of view. As with respect, humility does not require agreement on the point of view. But it does require the patience and forbearance to listen. It includes empathy—the capacity to sense what it might be like to be in the other's shoes.

Humility, for me, arises out of remembering God's greatness and his mercy and grace toward me. It arises from a deep sense that any challenge we confront pales in comparison to the chasm separating me from God. Yet God chose to bridge that chasm through the cross. Humility is also rooted in the knowledge that some aspect of your starting point—a fact, a perception, a misunderstanding—could be wrong. It isn't always wrong or presumed to be wrong. But it could be wrong because it is held by a human being. Humility is the antidote to the human tendency to think too highly of oneself and thus has a moderating effect on too much self-assurance and confidence.

Trustworthiness

Bridge builders are trustworthy. Trust is built by consistent action and by delivering agreed-upon results. It is built when I look out for someone—for their well-being and their dignity—even if they are not in the room. Trustworthiness is not built by talking behind someone's back nor by impugning their reputation, but rather by investigating all the facts before opining publicly. We build trust by giving someone the benefit of the doubt. Oftentimes, trustworthiness requires public restraint in order to fulfill a bridge-building role or calling.

Love

Building bridges is itself an act of love: love of neighbor, love of peace, love of God. But maintaining a posture of love in today's world requires more than willpower. It requires the Holy Spirit's power, because attempting to build bridges across deep divides results in fear—fear of getting it wrong, fear of angering powerful people who disagree with the bridge-building efforts, fear of damaging or losing one's reputation. But as the Bible reminds us, perfect love casts out all fear. So what does love look like? According to 1 Corinthians 13, love never gives up. Love cares for others more than self; it isn't envious or pushy, arrogant or me-first. Love doesn't fly off the handle or keep

THE BRIDGE BUILDER: SHIRLEY V. HOOGSTRA

account of wrongs. Instead, love takes pleasure in the truth. Love is patient, trusts God, looks for the best in others, never looks back, and is persistent to the end. Loving God and one's neighbor is not just a suggestion but an imperative for the Christian life. Bridge builders must develop enough self-awareness to determine whether they are operating out of love for others or a sense of fear of what they could lose. This is where having a community of faith and deep practices of spiritual health are essential. I use an app called Echo Prayer. In the areas that I find God has asked me to be a bridge builder, I set a reminder in this app so that I can pray about it regularly. I am painfully aware that promises I've made and intentions to pray can float right out of my mind. By using reminders, I keep before the Lord the work he has given me. I can bring before the Lord my heart so that I am guided and directed by him. It also fosters my desire to be respectful, open, humble, trustworthy, and loving. I am only able to love others when I am deeply connected to the God who is love.

None of these four qualities of bridge building is achieved overnight. And none is ever lived out perfectly. However, they can be learned and cultivated. And that learning and cultivation usually come from others who build bridges toward us.

Learning to Build Bridges

My mother's biggest contribution to my preparation as a bridge builder came in my teen years. My mother suffered at times from debilitating depression. Some of it came from grief—from a miscarriage, from the death of her brother. Some of it probably stemmed from the exhaustion and rigidity of being a housewife in the 1950s. Monday, wash. Tuesday, iron. Wednesday, clean. Thursday, grocery shop. Friday, bake.

My mother hid things well, and from the outside we looked like a normal Christian family. We attended every catechism, potluck supper, girls' club and boys' club, and school activity. We showed up for church twice on Sunday.

Things were different inside our home. My mother threatened at times to end her life, and her fatigue led to rages that frightened me. I learned I could be a calming influence that diverted her from her depression; I could read the room with precision and cheer her up. I learned not to be so afraid of her. I also learned that people are complex, both loving and scary. I learned that good things can happen when you lean into conflict rather than hide from it and that doing so is worth the risk.

Mom's depression lessened considerably later in life. She found a therapist. Dad retired. They did some projects together. Then, at age sixty-nine, she received a cancer diagnosis, and nine weeks later she was gone—"Gone to glory," as she would say. In those last days, she became intentionally reflective. She knew life had been really hard for her family at times, and in her hospital bed, she apologized to me. This was loving and brave of her, and I was able—as an adult who had made it pretty well past the chaos—to say to her, "Mom, all of you made all of me."

Influenced by my mom, I grew up and went to law school and started working as a divorce lawyer with families that were dissolving. I was sometimes asked how I could practice in this area as a Christian. I would respond, "Isn't this exactly where Christians should be—in the middle of the very hardest parts of the human story?" For most people, divorce is one of lowest points of their lives. Divorce includes feelings of failure, shame, grief, and anger. I listened to people at their lowest moments, showing them respect in the midst of their feeling of failure. I told them everyone has scars and bandages, and I told them it wasn't hopeless. I would suggest they consider counseling, and if that didn't work, I would journey with them in their shame and sadness.

I wanted my clients to feel my love for them as God loved them. They were broken, but their stories and lives could be put back together. I wanted to help them be honorable and generous even in the midst of hatred and fear. I wanted to model grace in the midst of chaos, because I *knew* grace in the midst of chaos. I now realize that God had used my childhood to equip me for this work. I had seen God's grace to my mother and father in the midst of my family's sadness, failure, and chaos. And I looked for every opportunity to share the gospel. In fact, I displayed the gospel story on my wall. A large John Swanson serigraph of "The Great Catch" hung in my office. It is a depiction of the disciples' miraculous catch of fish through the power and grace of Jesus (John 21). If the occasion presented itself, I would tell the story of Peter failing miserably as a friend and disciple when he denied Jesus three times. Yet Peter was offered a gift from Jesus, the great catch of fish. "I love you, Peter, even though you think you are unlovable and despised," Jesus said. I tried to be Jesus to those who felt unlovable and wounded.

Building Bridges in Our Communities

In my current role as the president of an association that represents Christian colleges and universities, I am once again presented with opportunities to build bridges across a number of contentious issues. One example is in the area of immigration reform. In 2012, President Obama issued regulations shielding from deportation some undocumented immigrants who were brought to the United States as children. Known as Deferred Action for Childhood Arrivals (DACA), some

Christians felt President Obama's order scoffed at the rule of law. How was it that people who broke the law, who did not follow the procedures set up for lawful entry, could reap a reward for their children? Wouldn't this actually encourage more people to disregard the policies and practices for proper immigration? Other Christians supported DACA and believed that how our laws treat the undocumented, the stranger or the vulnerable, is a reflection of our faith.

Many of the Christian colleges and universities I represent have undocumented persons as students. These students contribute through their work ethic, focus, and gratitude for the opportunity to study. They also live with daily uncertainty and fear because of their immigration status.

My organization has been part of a movement called the Evangelical Immigration Table. It promotes six principles: respect the God-given dignity of every person, protect the unity of the immediate family, respect the rule of law, secure national borders, ensure fairness to taxpayers, and establish a path toward legal status and/or citizenship for those who qualify and who wish to become permanent residents. Three years ago, as a newer leader of my organization, I recognized the competing interests and viewpoints in the immigration debate. But as the conversation surrounding immigration heated up, I had the opportunity to speak out on this issue. Keeping an open mind as a learner who respected varying viewpoints, I sought to get more information.

Fortunately, I was introduced to the Global Immersion Project. This organization educates people about conflict resolution and peacemaking in order to promote understanding. Immersion trips to Israel/Palestine and the Tijuana/San Diego border were our classroom. We confronted difficult questions that shaped our learning: "What would the world look like if the church took seriously our call to be peacemakers? What if peacemaking became a way of life?"

Given my responsibilities, I wanted to better understand the US border situation and DACA's impact. We met with a college-age woman who didn't know she was undocumented until receiving a full scholarship to a design college. Her parents then told her for the first time that she was not a citizen or legal resident and would be ineligible to accept it. She knew she was poor. She knew her parents were cautious. But she had been thriving in high school. She saw a future for herself in the country that was her home. And then it all changed. She was confronted with deception, despondency, and hopelessness. Her only recourse was to register under the DACA program, but doing so would put her family at risk because the registration required an address and other identifying information. In addition, what if the program went away? Were her ambitions for her future worth risking the security of her family? I listened. I was learning. Many questions moved through my own mind. What were her parents thinking? Why had they put her in this position? Couldn't our elected officials do better to figure this out? What should happen now? In the face of no easy answers, what do Christians do?

Later we met with border guards who presented their daily realities—cascading waves of humans who would do anything to get into the United States. Some asylum seekers. Some drug smugglers. The guards modeled dedication and felt frustration. Complexity abounded. We then crossed into Mexico and ate with the men in the Catholic homeless shelter in Tijuana. They spoke of being unexpectedly deported to an unfamiliar place, culture, and language. Their families remained in the United States. They felt shame, loneliness, and confusion. What hope did they have? Fortunately, the church was a bridge for them. A bridge that spanned one life behind them and one life in front of them.

I feel fortunate to be in this conversation, to be at this table. In my role, I argue for respect for undocumented people as image bearers of God. I try to replicate what Global Immersion modeled for me—not to be afraid of messy facts or competing interests. As a peacemaker and bridge builder, I want to have the openness and humility to take as long as needed to understand both sides of the story and then to act on behalf of the powerless, the poor, and the vulnerable.

Building Bridges to Find Common Ground

Another example of bridge building in my own life is Shannon Minter, a civil rights attorney and the legal director of the National Center for Lesbian Rights in San Francisco. We have many differences, but we are both lawyers. We are both passionate about our faith. We both want what's good for people. And we believe in the importance of finding common ground across our differences.

Shannon and I first met several years ago at a gathering at Yale Law School. We were participating in a symposium about religious liberty and human sexuality, a contentious topic in which sides frequently argue but rarely talk. But that weekend, the idea was to sit together to listen and discuss what each person thought were reasonable ideas to put on the table. It was a chance to model what John calls "confident pluralism." We wanted to explore how to live respectfully while holding to deeply divergent beliefs, to find common ground amid substantial difference. The conference modeled polite professional civility, yet I also sensed deep skepticism. On the one hand, Christian colleges and universities in my association sometimes felt attacked by progressives for our belief in traditional marriage and our commitment to religious mission. On the other hand, we heard painful stories of unjust discrimination from gay and lesbian participants at the conference.

During the conference, each of us was asked to describe our own perspectives but also to say what we feared most. It was a good question but a risky one. Progressives in the room talked about how they feared the continuing dignity-dismissing behavior especially prevalent in some religious communities. Conservatives talked about losing a way of life and the ability to teach their children their faith and about institutions being run out of existence. Both sides shared their perceptions of being disrespected, as well as their fears of metaphorical or actual extinction.

In the midst of this vulnerable encounter, I discovered Shannon to be a kind man and a fair person. He listened as I explained why Christian colleges needed exemptions when working with transgender students. When colleges have single-gender dorms or floors, moving a newly identifying transgender student from one side of the dormitory hall to the other side with a different gender was not so simple. Generally, these schools did not have dormitories where men and women cohabitated in the same room or on the same floor. Christian colleges maintained residence-life policies in a desire for men and women to honor and respect each other, and that goal was supported by having single-sex living spaces. Shannon paid attention. But he also presented his perspective as a legal advocate for LGBT students: that Christian colleges receiving public funds should not have many, if any, exemptions.

After the symposium concluded, I took the opportunity to thank Shannon for his candid remarks and for listening well. I mentioned that while our campuses wanted to treat transgender students well, it didn't always happen easily. He was struck by what he felt was my honesty and candor. He added that he had not realized the exemptions our colleges asked for had such practical reasons behind them. We had listened and heard each other well. Together, we built trust.

A few months later, we met unexpectedly in an airport. Over the next two hours we talked about how the two of us could facilitate understanding between transgender individuals and Christian institutions. It was an easy and natural conversation between two leaders who wanted their organizations to benefit the people they served. In their book *Leadership on the Line*, Ronald Heifetz and Marty Linsky say that leaders need to be motivated by love so that people's lives improve as a result of that leadership. Shannon wanted the transgender individuals he represented to have lives that were better and to stay connected, if possible, to their faith communities. And I wanted our Christian colleges to be able to retain their religious convictions and for students, faculty, and staff to understand gender dysphoria better. We both wanted students to be treated with understanding, charity, and care.

I found this bridge-building work deeply moving. It was profound to have found common ground to work toward instead of believing that a transgender advocate could be only an opponent. I saw the grace of God in operation in both my life and, by his report, in Shannon's life. When you only hear harsh and negative things said about you—both by LGBT activists toward religious people and religious people toward LGBT persons—it's not hard to experience fear and hatred, even if unarticulated. At points in our conversation, tears filled my eyes because my heart experienced a fuller knowledge of God's redemptive power. It's not often that you experience God so actively peeling away misunderstanding. Respect replaced distrust. While we became collaborators where we could agree, where we disagreed we knew we would be opponents—but with less fear, more respect, and greater love toward one another even on matters of deep difference. My life verse is 1 Peter 3:15: "Always be ready to make your defense to anyone who demands from you an accounting for the hope that is in you." My encounter with Shannon was a striking experience of the hope I have in Jesus Christ.

Bridge Building as Imitating Christ

Loving your neighbor is easiest when there's very little difference. Loving your neighbor is easiest when there are no contentious issues between you. Loving your neighbor is easiest when their lifestyle matches yours. Loving your neighbor is easiest when they believe like you do, vote like you do, shop where you do, have the same economic status you do, and send their children to the same schools you do. The smaller the gap between you, the easier the bridge is to build. The biggest *need* for bridge building, however, is where the gap is the biggest. Where you don't understand the other person or when you feel the other person might be your opponent or is even someone who hates you. Yet the degree of difficulty in loving our neighbor doesn't excuse us from loving that neighbor.

Paul instructed us in Ephesians, "Therefore be imitators of God, as beloved children, and live in love, as Christ loved us and gave himself up for us, a fragrant offering and sacrifice to God" (5:1–2). The call of bridge building is to imitate the love of Christ. We model that love when we extend ourselves across difference for the sake of understanding the other, when we demonstrate hope, when we bestow respect or dignity, and when we pursue reconciliation. Jesus spanned chasms to reconcile me to God. So if I try to span chasms, I am closer to being the Christ-imitator I want to be: loved by God and loving others for God's sake.

THE CAREGIVER

WARREN KINGHORN

IN JANUARY 1961, A YOUNG STUDENT AT IOWA STATE UNIVERSITY, Harvey Gantt, applied to transfer to the architecture program at Clemson University in South Carolina. His grades and test scores were well above average for incoming students, his application was compelling, and he was even a South Carolina resident. But Clemson repeatedly deferred, ignored, and blocked his application. Officially, this was done on procedural grounds, but the root cause was that Harvey Gantt was black. At the time, Clemson was an all-white institution, and the state of South Carolina wanted to keep it that way. But Gantt wanted change. He applied to Clemson anyway, then sued the university for his right to attend. His case made it to a federal appellate court, which ruled that Clemson had no grounds to deny admission in this case, clearing the way for Gantt to become Clemson's first black student in January 1963.[1] Gantt's legal team included distinguished civil rights lawyers Constance Baker Motley of the NAACP, fresh off her successful representation of James Meredith at the University of Mississippi, and Matthew J. Perry, who later became the first black South Carolinian to be appointed to a federal judgeship. Clemson hired a respected South Carolina lawyer named William Law Watkins.

I knew William Law Watkins as Granddaddy Bill.

I have inherited a lot from my grandfather. I share his height (before his death in 1999, we both stood at around six foot five), his love of learning and language, his lack of athleticism, and a little of his spirit. He loved his Presbyterian church, his community, and his family. When as children my younger brother and I worried about sleeping in my grandparents' home, Granddaddy Bill assured us that decades before, he had installed a "booger line" around the property and that no boogers, human or otherwise, would be able to harm us. We slept soundly. When we balked at eating scrambled eggs and grits, he sprinkled magic in our grits with an elaborate ritual and a twinkle in his eye. We cleaned our plates. When once we arrived at his house arguing bitterly with each other, he observed with raised eyebrows that we must have risen on the wrong side of the bed that morning. He escorted us to *his* bed, identified the wrong side and the right side of the bed, and required us to climb out on the right side of the bed. We complied, laughed, and stopped arguing. I remember him as an encourager and a gentle and peaceable man.

Later in his life, Granddaddy Bill would occasionally speak of his work in the Gantt case. Times were different then, he would say. He never expressed regret about defending Clemson. Segregation was the law of the land. But he said it was good that times had changed. He was proud of his role in ensuring that Gantt's eventual enrollment at Clemson was peaceful and orderly, unlike the violent and federally coerced desegregation of the flagship state universities in Mississippi and Alabama. And yet, if Granddaddy Bill had prevailed in his case in 1963, Harvey Gantt would not have been admitted to Clemson, and South Carolina would have remained the last state in the United States to resist integration.

The Gospel of Achievement and Competence

When I started public elementary school in Greenville, South Carolina, about thirty miles from Granddaddy Bill's home, Clemson University had been racially integrated for less than twenty years, and the public schools of my county had been integrated for only slightly more than a decade. But I was taught at school, at church, and at home to see slavery and segregation as unfortunate aspects of a settled past. Once, long ago, black and white children attended different schools and were unable to watch movies and play in the same parks together, but no more. The civil rights era had come, times had changed, and Martin Luther King Jr. had given a wonderful speech that people should be judged not by the color of their skin but by the content of their character. It was good that times had changed, I heard people say. Character, not color, mattered now.

And so I learned, from an early age, to cultivate my character: to respect my teachers and elders, to treat others fairly, and above all, to work hard and to study to show myself "approved by [God]" (2 Tim. 2:15). "God has given you gifts," adults at church and school said. "Be sure to use them. Maybe you are called to be a preacher, or a doctor." I came to love God as a generous gift-giver and as a demanding taskmaster, one who would liberally dispense talents but throw into outer darkness his servants who wasted them. I prayed the Sinner's Prayer, invited Jesus into my heart, and was baptized when I was seven years old. Jesus was my Savior, and I would be going to heaven. But I believed that what I did with my life was largely a matter of my own effort and determination, and I had better not screw it up.

I accepted that I was white and financially secure, and understood that racism lived on—not in racist structures and systems but in the unfortunate beliefs and actions of individual racists. But I didn't think that race and class mattered for the opportunities I would have or for the kind of person I was becoming. What mattered was my status as saved before God, my God-given gifts, and my willingness to work hard. I believed that anyone, if they worked hard enough, could succeed. While I noticed that my middle and high school classes were whiter and filled with kids from families of means as I moved into more honors and Advanced Placement courses, this never occurred to me to be a problem of justice. It was just the way things were.

I left South Carolina in my early twenties, and for the past two decades have lived and worked in the world of research universities, first as a student at Harvard Medical School and then as a resident in psychiatry, a graduate student in theology, and now a professor at Duke. In many ways I am living out those hopes that were declared over me. Though I am not a preacher, at least not an ordained one, I am an elder at my church and teach as a theologian in a Christian seminary. And I *am* a doctor, a psychiatrist, who cares for patients and who teaches psychiatry to others.

The world of the university, and especially the world of medicine, was made by and for people like me—people who thrive on the twin values of achievement and competence. These values lead to a false gospel, and like any false gospel, they always demand more. The culture of research universities is always *more*: more publications, more grants, more awards, higher rankings, more course offerings, more students. Research universities run on *more*. The culture of academic medicine also offers a ready-made ladder of achievement that never ends. There is always one more rung to climb, one more discovery to make, one more paper to write, one more treatment to learn or to develop.

As I progressed through medical training, I loved the way it rewarded achievement and competence. I knew that structure and thrived in it. I also celebrated the way I believed this structure provided a straightforward path for diversity among medical practitioners. One of the remarkable things about modern medicine, including modern American psychiatry, is that its language and practices are so standardized that people from virtually anywhere in the world can learn them. Each year my own institution, Duke University Medical Center, welcomes women and men of many racial and ethnic backgrounds from all over the world to work and learn, and in very short order they are putting these differences aside as they share a common purpose of caring for people who are sick. This makes hospitals and medical training programs, not unlike scientific research laboratories, energetically diverse spaces. I love this diversity and this shared purpose.

I also value the way medicine allowed me, as a physician, to enter into the lives of patients who were different from me, and yet to understand them in standardized ways that did not require me to know all of the details of their histories. In medicine, physicians get to know their patients through a highly determined, ritualized form known as the "H&P"—the history and physical. The point of the H&P is to learn and to present information in a structured way that gets to the point of why patients are seeking medical care and how best to help them. Physicians are taught from the earliest stages of medical training to gather a chief complaint, followed by a history of present illness that tells a brief background story of this chief complaint. This is followed by sections devoted to past medical history, allergies, medications, and family history, with a section on social history to gather basic information about housing, relationships, finances, and other issues that might be relevant to the chief complaint. These accounts are followed by a documentation of the physical examination (as well as, in psychiatry, a mental status examination), an assessment, and finally a plan. Though institutions and clinicians may add sections or modify them for particular purposes, every physician anywhere in the United

States and likely anywhere in the world is familiar with this form. The H&P allows for a standard and straightforward way of describing patients that foregrounds their medical problems over the rest of their identity—so that, for example, a "fifty-eight-year-old man with history of diabetes mellitus type 2, hyperlipidemia, and hypertension presenting with new-onset chest pain" can be a homeless person or a US senator—in theory to be treated the same.

Psychiatrists have long debated whether mental illness should be treated this way, but by the time I learned psychiatry, the field had committed itself to this medical model. Psychiatrists follow a guidebook, the *Diagnostic and Statistical Manual of Mental Disorders*, or DSM, that lists hundreds of diagnostic categories—like major depressive disorder, bipolar disorder, and post-traumatic stress disorder—and describes each of these categories with a list of characteristic experiential and behavioral symptoms. When psychiatrists and other clinicians use the DSM, as virtually all health systems and insurance plans require, we diagnose patients with mental illness by establishing that they meet the criteria (usually a certain number of items on a checklist) for a particular mental disorder category. There are pros and cons to this approach to diagnosis, but a practical advantage is that, like other physicians, psychiatrists can engage with patients with whom we have little in common and can come to understand them in standardized ways that foreground their medical problems over the rest of their identity.

Long before I became a physician, I had been pursuing achievement and competence, and modern academic medicine seemed to offer the best of all possible worlds. I found myself immersed in a prestigious and highly valued system that celebrated and rewarded accomplishment and ability. Further, by embracing standardized approaches to diagnosis and treatment, modern medicine makes this achievement attainable: being a good doctor in a system that embraces standardization is primarily a matter of knowing the right things, and I was certainly capable of that. This was made all the more rewarding by the fact that as a psychiatrist I was helping suffering people decrease their pain and live more productively and was being given credit by both patients and colleagues for doing so. Even better, medicine's standardized approaches made it possible for me to work with a racially and culturally diverse set of colleagues and to care for racially and culturally diverse patients, in ways that affirmed that though I might be a white American man, I had left racism behind.

All of this squared perfectly with my identity as a Christian. Achievement and competence became core to the gospel, marks of my Christian commitment, a way to work out my salvation with fear and trembling (Phil. 2:12). Jesus was a healer, and as a caregiver I was participating in the healing ministry of Jesus. Studying medicine, I was learning to appreciate how "fearfully and wonderfully made" human beings are (Ps. 139:14), and to stand in awe at God's creation. By caring for patients and working with colleagues from different racial and cultural backgrounds, I was even working to promote a colorblind society in which everyone had opportunities to give and to receive medical care and, therefore, to thrive. If I was being lauded and rewarded for this work, with both money and status, then all the better: it was a happy example of how, even in an unredeemed world, "by knowledge the rooms are filled with all precious and pleasant riches" (Prov. 24:4).

Losing Faith

The straightforward and comforting narrative that modern medicine is a force for good that is capable of healing not only disease but also social division and injustice, and that is available to anyone willing to work sufficiently hard to master it, is a lovely story. It is also a false story. It wasn't long into my training as a physician that I began to notice the holes in the narrative.

I was exposed to one of these holes during a Christian retreat in medical school. After I casually lauded the racial diversity of our Christian student group, an African American classmate responded, "I'm from inner-city Baltimore, and when you grow up in inner-city Baltimore, you learn that the world is not for you." I was stunned. How could a successful Harvard medical student say this? I had always experienced the world as basically *for* me. What would it feel like to grow up living in a world that is *not* for you? Though I was then in my twenties, I was able to hear as if for the first time my colleague's experience of growing up black and poor in the United States, and her ongoing experiences of racism, in a way that upended my long-entrenched conceptions of a colorblind society.

Since then, though my older habits have never died and I think that I still miss more than I understand, I've learned to hear and to see a lot more. I've learned how the Tuskegee Study of Untreated Syphilis in the Negro Male—in which the US Public Health Service watched black men suffer and die of syphilis for decades rather than giving them inexpensive and effective antibiotic treatment—was a symbol of the negative experiences and distrust that many African Americans have had within US health care as a whole. I've heard an African American pastor in Durham gently but firmly say to me, upon learning that I worked at Duke University Medical Center and reflecting on Duke's legacy as a white research institution that practiced segregated care for the first few decades of its existence, "Most people in my congregation would rather die than go to Duke." I've heard stories of black physician colleagues being commonly mistaken for nursing assistants or custodians. I have encountered research that even now physicians in training often underestimate the degree to which black patients are in pain relative to white patients.[2]

Though I still value the racial and cultural diversity of modern health care and believe that most physicians do not want to be racist, I now understand that racism runs deeper than the conscious beliefs of individuals. Racism, like sin in general, is embedded in institutions and structures that operate through us, even when we're not aware of them. It is not enough for me to not want to be racist and to try to treat everyone with dignity—though of course that is a necessary start. I must, rather, ask myself—and, more importantly, invite others to ask of me—how my life has been shaped within particular racial structures and assumptions and how my actions and inactions either perpetuate or heal deep structures of racial injustice and inequality.

To start, that means owning and loving the fact that I am my grandfather's grandson. Granddaddy Bill was a loving and decent man, *and* his legal work defended a segregated racial order that was and is deeply sinful and contrary to the gospel. The contradictions of his life run deep in my own identity. That he was no different from many other white professional men of his time only adds to the urgency of claiming my identity as his grandson. I have come to see that the gifts I bear from him cannot ultimately be abstracted from his place, and mine, in the racial order that he defended. A frugal man, he never earned a high income but saved and invested money throughout his life, and he generously supported the education of his eight grandchildren. His wealth—including, perhaps, part of what Clemson University paid him to represent it against Harvey Gantt—helped fund my education at Harvard Medical School.

In less tangible ways, I have benefited all of my life from being born into a family for whom college education and financial security are assumed norms, encouraged by generations of straightforward access to white-dominated networks and institutions. I cannot live faithfully as a Christian now, nor practice faithfully as a physician, unless I allow that reality to sink in, accepting both its gifts and its weight. The gift of feeling (more or less) at home at Duke University cannot be separated from the weight of knowing that Duke, like nearly every other elite American research university, was founded to serve and to perpetuate a social and economic class of educated white men who looked very much like me. The gift of not having to justify my identity and existence as a doctor cannot be separated from the weight of knowing that many physician friends and colleagues—not only physicians of color but also physicians who are women—experience obstacles related to distrust and injustice that add undue burden to the already challenging work of medicine. Because I am my grandfather's grandson, I cannot live as if my own experience is not bound up with theirs.

Second, more broadly, I began to lose faith that modern medicine is always a force for good that leads people toward health. Though we doctors, nurses, and other clinicians work within "health care systems" and often describe ourselves as "health care providers," it turns out that American "health care" has no clear, definable standard of health to govern its practices. I came to see many examples where medical practices led not to health in any holistic sense but to complex and technologically dominated progressions of suffering and disease. As a student I saw people suffering for weeks or months in intensive care units, near death and with little possibility of recovery, but with family members or clinicians or both pushing to keep the body's organs functioning. In these cases, the patient's care was often dominated by the urgent imperative to "do something"—and I learned that if asked to "do something," modern medicine will nearly always come up with something technological to do, however invasive and marginally beneficial.

I also saw more subtle and pervasive forms of focusing on disease rather than on patients' overall health in my own field of psychiatry. I began to see that the standardized, structured diagnoses of the DSM, intended to enable clinicians to understand patients in straightforward ways, could be ways of *not* seeing what mattered most. In my work with combat veterans, for instance, I began to realize that while the DSM diagnosis of post-traumatic stress disorder (PTSD) had conditioned me to understand trauma as a disorder driven by fear, what many veterans struggled with most deeply was not fear but rather guilt and shame for things done or not done in war—a phenomenon now known as "moral injury." If I really took their stories seriously, and really engaged this guilt and shame on its own terms, I would have to practice psychiatry differently, focusing less on symptom reduction by any means possible (including with medication), and more on understanding what war was like for them—something that would take me well outside the comfort zone of standardized diagnosis and therapy. I began to see that psychiatry's standardized approach to diagnosis might make the work of psychiatrists more efficient but could get in the way of understanding patients' stories in a manner that would lead to genuine healing. And this, I came to see, was not unrelated to race and racism; many studies, for example, have found that physicians using standardized diagnoses tend to assign more stigmatizing diagnoses such as schizophrenia to black patients, relative to white patients.[3] In all of this, I began to see how medicine, far from a benign force for good and healing, could serve as what the Bible refers to as a "power," defined as a "structuring structure" of life in a fallen world that, while at its best a force for good, could just as easily obscure or hide the good, and even contribute to evil.[4]

Finally, and more personally, I lost faith in my own ability to work out my own salvation through achievement and competence. It turned out that the values that undergirded my Christian self-understanding, and that worked so beautifully in my educational and professional life, did not work so well for friendships or for marriage. At one point in my mid-twenties I found myself both professionally successful and miserably lonely, too focused on pursuing "whatever is true, whatever is honorable, whatever is just" (Phil. 4:8) to allow any mortal human being to make a significant claim on me. Insecure and afraid of judgment, I found it difficult to entrust myself and my fears fully to others. Grace pursued me and found me, almost sacramentally, in the patience and love of my wife, who has gently and often painfully helped me begin to understand what it means to love, what it means to be vulnerable, what it means to be human. As I transitioned from a single person to a husband, and then to a father, I have learned that being a Christian is not ultimately about mastery and control, either of myself or of others or of the world, but about embracing the vulnerability, dependence, and love that comes with living inside the life of Jesus, embraced by the Father through the power of the Holy Spirit as God's beloved child, and resting there.

Walking with Wounded Wayfarers

Every day I still feel the power and pull of the gospel of achievement and competence. It continues to permeate the world of health care and, especially, the world of research universities. But it is a false gospel, one rooted in control rather than wonder, and one that paints a theologically, psychologically, and historically false picture of who human beings are. The gospel of achievement and competence, with its promise of individual sanctification through hard work and success, is not the good news Jesus proclaimed. It is, rather, the false gospel of a culture that values productivity and efficiency above all else. It forms abstracted, universal individuals who believe ourselves to transcend place, culture, and history in order to achieve socially determined markers of success. It promotes standardized language and practices, like the DSM in psychiatry, that render success a matter of knowledge and technical skill rather than attunement to one's place and its people. It rewards and reinforces the power of status-granting institutions like universities, media organizations, companies, and maybe even churches. Through all of this, similar to the ways John mentions in his chapter, I believe that it is a characteristically American gospel. And insofar as this American gospel focuses on the individual, ignores the claims of place, culture, and history, and allows us to proceed without engaging racism's history or racism's lingering wounds, it is a characteristically white gospel—a false white gospel that obscures, rather than reveals, the good news of Jesus.

As I have gradually begun to recognize the grip that the gospel of achievement and competence has had on my life, and as I walk as a psychiatrist alongside people who are suffering the costs of that false gospel—either because they are themselves also in its grip or because they have been cast aside by it as those who are neither competent nor successful—I have begun to understand humans and myself in different ways. I offer here five affirmations about what it means to be human.

1. We Are Rooted in Place, Culture, and History

I had not practiced psychiatry long when I realized that if I used only standardized diagnostic language to understand and to speak with my patients—as long as I know a patient as only "a fifty-eight-year-old man with major depressive disorder and PTSD"—I could generate a technically competent assessment and plan but know almost nothing of patients as human beings. In the same way, if Christians speak to each other only in abstract theological language—*You are a sinner. God loves you and sent Jesus to forgive your sin. Accept his grace and live in freedom*—then we can speak truthfully, and yet know almost nothing about each other. To know each other, to know ourselves, we have to be specific.

For me, this has meant owning the fact that I am a white man from Greenville, South Carolina, the grandson of William Law Watkins and three other equally formative grandparents, loved and formed in Greenville's public schools and in a white evangelical Southern Baptist church. The racial and cultural history of South Carolina, of Southern Baptists, and of my family have formed me into who I am. Though I can seek to better understand that formation and try to name its blessings and its challenges, I can no more deny or ignore it than I can deny or ignore myself. But I have found that this desire to understand my own history and my own formation, far from a retreat into some sort of "identity politics," has helped me relate more humanly to others, including others who look and speak very unlike me who are also rooted in place, culture, and history, and who have been forced to be more aware of that than I, as a white American man, have ever been encouraged to be.

2. We Find Ourselves in Relationship

Researchers who study human development have long understood that none of us are isolated individuals. Humans—beginning before birth and continuing throughout life—are built for relationship and need relationship. The set of capacities and skills that we associate with having a "self"—the capacities to distinguish oneself from others, to feel and name emotion and belief, to reflect on our experience, to act with purpose—all emerge in the relational bonds between mother and child, father and child, caregiver and child, children with each other.

Never individuals, we *find* ourselves in relationship. Others reflect us to ourselves and allow us to discover who we are. Relationships are key to our happiness, to our sense of meaning and purpose, to our self-identity.

Having been formed in the gospel of achievement and competence, I struggle to seek out relationships that are not somehow related to productivity. But I have learned that it is not in knowledge or technique, but in sharing life with others, that I become more human. I am learning to make time and space for the relationships that matter, beginning with my wife. But I am also finding as a psychiatrist that the quality of my relationship with my patients is at least as important for their healing and recovery as are any of my techniques. It is easy to think of outpatient physicians as vehicles for prescriptions and procedures that are themselves the *real* source of healing; doctors, in this way of thinking, are basically overpaid prescription vending machines. But when I am able to develop relationships with patients in which they trust me (and vice versa), in which we are able to speak truthfully to each other, and in which we are able to discern together what is most important in treatment, this is healing for patients and energizing for me. Patients feel less alone, more willing to be open and vulnerable, and less likely to focus on suicide as a means of escape. In some cases, they are able reduce the number and dose strength of medications. And beyond simply making patients feel comfortable to discuss treatment options, there is evidence that a strong therapeutic alliance between prescribing clinicians and patients actually helps psychiatric medications to work more effectively.[5]

3. We Carry Wounds and Will Go to Great Lengths to Avoid Shame

There are good reasons why we humans commonly attempt to distance ourselves from place, culture, and history, and seek either to avoid or control relationships. Place, culture, history, and relationship, because they are so powerful and important, are often the sites of our deepest wounds. As a psychiatrist and also as a teacher, I have learned that psychological wounds that I used to assume were rare—such as the wounds that arise from childhood sexual abuse, childhood physical abuse, intimate partner violence, and rape—are in fact quite common, collectively affecting over 20 percent of Americans. And all of us, even if we have not lived through these forms of trauma, carry wounds that leave us fearful or detached or ashamed in particular areas of our lives.

I have learned in myself, and by walking with others, that shame in particular is an intensely powerful and universal emotion that, because of its power, both motivates us and destroys us. As psychiatrist Curt Thompson has named, shame sends the message, "You are not enough," and, "If others really knew you, you would be abandoned and rejected."[6] My own worlds of health care and the research university use shame as lubricant and fuel for the culture of *more*. The messages that "you are not smart enough, you are not productive enough, you are not well-read enough" encourage me to do what humans characteristically do when faced with shame: to withdraw into a protective shell (accepting the shame-judgment and hoping not to be found out), to blame and shame others or "the system" (rejecting the shame-judgment by deflecting it), or to work harder and harder (accepting the shame-judgment but hoping to prove to others that it is wrong). None of these strategies works very well over the course of a lifetime, and yet I feel them in myself and see them in others all the time.

Because shame is so aversive and it is often more tolerable to feel other emotions like fear, sadness, and especially anger, I have learned to look for shame as a root when people are treating each other badly.

When a system—whether that system is a congregation, a clinic, or Congress—seems to be trapped in a self-destructive pattern where people are acting aggressively and even irrationally toward each other, it is helpful to attend to that system's ecology of shame. In the same way, I often wonder how shame affects the way that white Americans like me engage what Wendell Berry has called the "hidden wound" of racism in white people.[7] The knowledge that my grandfather actively participated in defending segregation, and the knowledge that as a white man I benefit whether I want to or not from unjust legacies of racial privilege, can all too easily lead me to withdraw into a protective shell (e.g., staying in mostly white spaces or attending only to media that does not challenge me), to blame and shame others (e.g., by heaping scorn on overt racists or by dismissing talk of structural racism as "identity politics"), or to work harder and harder to signal to others that I am not a racist. White Christian responses to race in the United States commonly take one of these three forms.

4. We Are Loved, Known, and Beautiful

The gospel of achievement and competence, by grounding our value as humans in our productivity, efficiency, and self-sufficiency, encourages us to ignore or deny whatever stands in the way of our capacity for production—including our wounds and our bonds of place, culture, history, and relationship. By encouraging us to ignore or deny these core dimensions of our embodied humanness, while also teaching that we are worthy insofar as we are productive and are not excessively dependent on others, the gospel of achievement and competence delivers us ever more tightly into the grip of shame. But the gospel of Jesus Christ starts and ends in a fundamentally different place. Our dignity as humans does not come from how hard we work, or where we are from, or what we produce, or how capable we are of any activity. It comes, rather, from the fact that as God's good creatures, we are loved and known by God. "You hem me in, behind and before," the psalmist wrote. "Such knowledge is too wonderful for me; it is so high that I cannot attain it" (Ps. 139:5–6). God's love for us, God's intimate knowledge of us, God's adoption of us as children in the body and life of Jesus, is unattainable by us and yet graciously given to us, a gift that precedes any of our knowing or doing. It is also a powerful cure for shame.

The philosopher Josef Pieper once remarked that at the root of love is the affirmation, "It's good that you exist; it's good that you are in this world!"[8] I am able to escape the gospel of achievement and competence only when I accept that regardless of what I can or can't do, it is good that I exist. I can help and care for my patients only when I convey to them, explicitly or implicitly, "It's good that you exist!" And I am able to own and love myself as a southern white evangelical Christian man, my grandfather's grandson, bearer of complicated legacies of privilege, only when I remember that my deepest identity is not in my whiteness but inside the body of a brown-skinned Middle Eastern man who died, rose, and ascended because he loves me as himself. In Jesus, I know that I am called both to honor those parts of my formation that introduced him to me, and also to die to all that is not "created according to the likeness of God in true righteousness and holiness," including racial privilege (Eph. 4:24). I'm still learning how to sort these two things apart, and I don't always get it right. I still have a lot of dying to do. But I know that the security of Jesus' love is the only place to start.

5. We Are Wayfarers

Images of journey and pilgrimages run through Scripture. "Since we are surrounded by so great a cloud of witnesses," the author of

Hebrews encouraged us, "let us also lay aside every weight and the sin that clings so closely, and let us run with perseverance the race that is set before us, looking to Jesus the pioneer and perfecter of our faith" (12:1–2). As humans, we are always wayfarers. We journey *from* God (our Source and Creator) and *to* God (our end and our joy), a return that is made possible by our participation in the life of Jesus. But the journey is hard, and we sometimes grow weary, or take wrong turns, or experience illness or injury, or find ourselves in land that is unfamiliar and even hostile. At these times, and others, we need fellow wayfarers to walk alongside us, asking us and helping us to answer, "What is needed, right now, for the journey?"

This question, "What is needed, right now, for the journey?" is central to my own understanding of myself as a Christian. It is also central to how I walk with others as a caregiver. For some of my patients, what's needed is medication or some other medical technology. But for many others, what's most needed is a job, or a place to live, or friendship, or freedom from an abusive context. For others, it's forgiveness. For still others, it's being welcomed into a community. Approaching my patients as wayfarers, and seeing myself as a wayfarer privileged to walk with them, forces me out of a posture of control and expertise, and into a posture of humility and respect, attending as closely as I can to their stories rather than to their symptoms alone.

Caregiving with Gospel Confidence (and Joy)

Granddaddy Bill was a connoisseur and lover of good stories. In his later years he would repeat detailed stories told to him a half-century earlier and laugh as if he were hearing them for the first time. He wrote meticulous histories of his county and of his church because he believed that you can know and love a place and people only when you know its stories. In this, he was certainly right. Stories, as Lecrae explains in his chapter, shape our vision of the world.

For much of my life, I lived the gospel of achievement and competence, the story that I could succeed as a human and as a caregiver by working hard and by attaining the right credentials, knowledge, and skill. That story still grips me. It also impoverishes me, and it renders me less faithful as a Christian living in today's complex world. I am finding life and joy, though, in a larger story, one in which I am a wayfarer loved and known by God, called not to control but to wonder, and called to walk alongside fellow wayfarers.

This larger story teaches me that I am loved and known by God not because of what I can do but simply because it is so—and this is the ultimate ground of the confidence and competence that I have as a caregiver. Because of this larger story of God's love in Jesus, I am learning to know and love others *and myself* not as abstractions but as human beings who are rooted in place and culture and history.

Gospel confidence comes when Christians are so secure in the love of God that we can get close to the ground of our own lives and our own histories, the sin and the trauma that our lives and histories carry—to know that *even there* we are loved and that *from there* we can change and heal. It comes when we can attend to shame rather than avoiding or denying it. It comes when we can say to one another, even those very different from us, "It's good that you exist. It's good that you are in this world!"—and show that we mean it by the way we live in the world. And it comes when we remember that whoever we are and whatever we have done, we have been folded by grace into Jesus' body (1 Tim. 1:12–17). It is there, in Jesus' life and not in our own achievement and competence, that we are granted the faith and love that we need to walk justly together.

THE RECONCILER

TRILLIA NEWBELL

EVERY DAY WHEN I WAKE UP, I AM REMINDED OF THE
fractures in this world. Whether it's the distant memory of a past
relationship or the quick glance at social media, I am confronted with
the reality that people are divided and often immersed in strife. The
greatest reminder for me, however, is nothing external to me; it is that
I wake up each morning with milky brown skin. This skin is crafted
by my Creator God, and for it I am grateful. It is also skin that leads
to bigotry, prejudice, and discrimination.

But God has called me to be a reconciler.

A reconciler is one who does the work of reconciliation: restor-
ing friendships, bringing harmony, resolving differences. My life and
work have been focused on the ministry of reconciliation. For me this
task has meant learning to be forbearing, forgiving, and patient while
speaking the truth in love.

I grew up in the South with two parents who experienced far more
blatant racism and hatred than I have known, but who taught us to love
others regardless of what they might say about us. I wouldn't say I grew
up in a Christian home, but I did grow up in a loving home. And it's
that common-grace love for others that my parents instilled in me that

gave me a desire to see people live in harmony with one another. I figured I could either be a part of the solution or part of the problem, and I have sought as much as humanly possible to be a part of the solution. It hasn't always been easy and I've failed at times, but our call to reconciliation is a part of what it means to image God—and it's worth it.

As a teenager I learned about the civil rights movement and the brave men and women who endured pain, suffering, and sometimes even death for defending the rights of others. I watched footage of Rodney King being dragged out of his car and beaten by police officers who were later acquitted of charges of excessive force—an acquittal that sparked devastating riots that in turn led to King's famous plea, "Can't we all just get along?"[1] I marched in our city's civil rights parade every January as we celebrated the birthday of Martin Luther King Jr.

And I have painful personal memories, such as the time a mom explained to me why her son couldn't date a black girl—because we were different. She wrapped her explanation in sentiments such as "You are kind" and "You are free to be his friend," but our difference in skin color was too much for her to bear. The thought of her son dating me was disgraceful; in her mind, it was "not right." Not right because to her, I was a different kind of person, an alien of sorts, a sub-creature. She didn't use these words, but her repeated stressing of our differences made it clear that something about me wasn't the same as her family and her people, and my kind of different wasn't good enough for her son. This was a hard pill for me to swallow as a teenager, but one I became accustomed to receiving.

During my college years, I had the opportunity to be the co-director of diversity affairs for our college student government. I helped host a few events we called Coffee Talks, open to anyone on campus willing to discuss race. Those discussions were helpful and eye opening, but they only scratched the surface.

I'll never forget sitting in my senior political science class when a young white man shared his disgust and concern that black people might get into law school ahead of him because of quotas and affirmative action. Through tears I responded that not only had I gotten into law schools but I was an honor student and had done well enough on my LSAT to get in. To assume that every black person who got into law school did so because of affirmative action was appalling at best, racist at worst.

If you met me, you might laugh to know that I have been racially profiled. At five foot two and 120 pounds, I'm not much of a threat. But this hasn't stopped some people from assuming the worst of me based on the color of my skin. I'm only scratching the surface of my experience. You could speak to most African Americans and find similar stories of racial bias, racism, and discrimination.

But I am called to be a reconciler.

Growing up, I attended church only on major holidays. I found a church during my junior year in high school, but I discovered that it was not gospel-focused. When I decided to leave, the members responded with cruelty rather than love, harassing me and letting me know that I was doomed to hell for not entrusting myself to them and their way of living. Before long, I said goodbye to church and vowed never to return. I didn't want to have anything to do with organized religion.

But that was not God's plan, and it would be God's plan that would transform my understanding of reconciliation.

It was the summer of 1998, right before my sophomore year in college. I was going to be a camp leader, as many college students are during the summer, and I was even going to have an assistant. They said her name was Marcy.[2] She arrived at camp with her blonde ponytail swinging, her blue eyes shining, her bubbly spirit infectious. It was easy to believe that she was a few years younger than I. Not that she was immature—she wasn't—but there was an innocence about her that poured out as she spoke and interacted with the campers.

She would be instrumental in changing the whole course of my life.

Marcy and I were polar opposites. I was black and she was white. I was in college and studious, and she had decided to leave college early to do campus ministry. Later I would find out that she came from a fairly wealthy family, while mine would have been considered lower-middle class. Most important, she was a Christian, and I definitely was not.

Our first night of camp, Marcy plopped down on her bed, broke open a Bible, and began reading quietly to herself. My guard went up immediately. "What are you doing?" I asked. She explained she was "having quiet time."

I was not excited to see that opened Bible on her bed. Up to that point, I had not had a great experience with Christians. In addition to my painful church experience in high school, I remembered going to a summer Vacation Bible School day with a friend and having the children look at me strangely. The teacher had basically ignored the few black children in the place, and when we all gathered in the church she had stuck us in the back.

That night at camp I ended up sharing these painful memories with Marcy. By the end of the night, my new friend and I were both crying over my past church experience and my fears—and she had also shared the gospel of salvation with me.

After that summer, Marcy and I would meet together every now and then, but it took me some time before I agreed to go to church with her. Then finally, in the spring of 2000, after a broken engagement and humiliation over my sin, I visited her church. And I stayed.

I remember that Sunday morning like it was yesterday. While we were singing "Rock of Ages," the Lord began to soften my heart and reveal his grace to me. After the church service, Marcy and two others prayed for me, and I was saved.

Jesus, the Reconciler

Sometime after that Sunday experience, I read Ephesians 2:8–9: "For by grace you have been saved through faith, and this is not your own doing; it is the gift of God—not the result of works, so that no one may boast." I thought, *That's it! That's what happened.* The Lord hadn't saved me because of anything I had done or anything I could ever do. It happened by his grace, by his free gift, by his own power! I was in need of being reconciled to God. And Jesus did that work of reconciliation (Rom. 5:10–11).

What struck me about my friend who shared the gospel with me was that she wasn't at all concerned that I was black and older and the leader of the camp. None of that mattered to her. She was an evangelist and loved to share with those who were not like her. Motivated by love, she shared the gospel with me, and the course of my whole life was changed—*forever.*

I'll always be grateful for Marcy's loving outreach. And yet she was not the one who reconciled me to God. She was a vessel the Lord used, but ultimately it was the work of Jesus that made that reconciliation possible. It is his work on the cross that allows us to be reconciled to one another.

Throughout the Gospels, Jesus related to people who were different from him, even people who might have been considered enemies—tax collectors, for example, or Samaritans, who were hated by the Jewish people and vice versa.[3]

He was bold to share, bold to the point of his own death on a cross, because of his love for souls. And with his death came the reconciliation of all people. Jesus tore the veil of hostility:

> For he is our peace; in his flesh he has made both groups into one and has broken down the dividing wall, that is, the hostility between us. He has abolished the law with its commandments and ordinances, that he might create in himself one new humanity in place of the two, thus making peace, and might reconcile both groups to God in one body through the cross, thus putting to death that hostility through it. (Eph. 2:14–16)

As Kristen explains more fully in her chapter, the reality for Christians is that we are already spiritually united and reconciled to one another in Christ Jesus. Our problem and trouble is that we don't live out our reality. But beyond our relationship to one another as Christians, we are called to be reconcilers in this world.

The gospel has power to bring even the most unlikely of people together for God's glory. "For I am not ashamed of the gospel; it is the power of God for salvation to everyone who has faith, to the Jew first and also to the Greek" (Rom. 1:16).

Our Call to Be Reconcilers

Since becoming a Christian, I have realized that the things my parents taught me growing up and the ways I longed for unity and oneness among others were all part of a common-grace, image-bearing impulse. My father taught his daughters to love and forgive those who wronged us. He taught us that unity was possible, and that all those who had gone before us in the civil rights movement had fought a good fight.

I came to realize that these longings for love, forgiveness, justice, and unity reflected our Creator. And once I had accepted Christ, what had once been a mere social desire and pursuit for me became a conviction bolstered by Scripture. But my pursuit of and desire for reconciliation didn't become easier once I became a Christian. In many ways, it became harder, and the revelation of just how far we have to go became almost paralyzing.

A few years ago, I wrote a book called *United: Captured by God's Vision for Diversity*, which gives a short theology of race, shares my testimony, and lays out the benefits of diverse friendships.[4] With that I entered the Christian public race conversation, and I did so with a bit of naïveté. Although I knew our churches were mostly segregated, I didn't believe that divide was actually driven by racism or the sin of partiality. The next few years opened my eyes.

Most Christians I met were content with the status quo, and I found that the race conversation had barely reached the church. I was met with a resistance I wasn't expecting. It wasn't always blatant, though. Most of the time it looked a lot like apathy. But it was real . . . and daunting. We can't love our neighbor if we don't care about their suffering.

The years following were painful as I realized in greater ways that the pain and suffering of many black and brown people was not a major priority for the church. But God was gracious to remind me that Genesis 3 ruined our relationships with one another, and this continues to play out in so many ways, from issues of race to socioeconomic factors to the challenge of serving those unlike us in experience and season of life. It takes work for any of us to focus on someone other than ourselves.

Actually, I realized it takes more than that. We simply cannot be reconcilers without first recognizing our collective need for Jesus.

So I had to make a choice: be an ambassador for Jesus or not. This, I believe, is the first step. You and I have to realize that we are ambassadors, and as ambassadors we represent in both word and deed someone greater than ourselves.

I've never been given the title ambassador. I just have been a part of enough groups to know that I am unofficially representing the organization or church or family by way of membership.

But as a Christian, I do have that title. The Word of God tells us that we have been reconciled to God and, therefore, we are ambassadors for Christ: "God is making his appeal through us" (2 Cor. 5:20). We have been given a treasure, and we are called to share it, display it, keep it, and walk in it. Being an ambassador helps you and me be reconcilers. As we recognize this new reality, we will be eager to do the work of the Lord. But before we can truly do our work as ambassadors, we must understand why we have been called to this.

Because I didn't become a Christian until the age of twenty-two, I had a lot of time before that to fall into grievous sin. So when I finally understood the gospel, there were no sweeter words I could hear than those that told me I was a new creation. Anyone who places his or her trust and faith in the Lord is a new creation (v. 17). The old has passed away. That's great news to a sinner like me—and that's great news for a sinner like you. And to know that this is all from God, that he has renewed us through and by the sacrificial blood of Jesus, is truly amazing grace (v. 19).

Oh, what love is this: "For our sake he made him to be sin who knew no sin, so that in him we might become the righteousness of God" (v. 21). This exchange is why we sing "amazing grace!" Grace truly is amazing!

And so, because of our understanding of the gospel, we are controlled by the love of Christ (v. 14). The love of Christ motivates us to be ambassadors, which leads to a ministry of reconciliation (v. 18). It is the love of Christ that moves us to regard others not according to the flesh but according to the Spirit (v. 16).

The implications of our faith and our role as ambassador for Christ change everything about the way we live. Or at least they should. We know that we live in a fallen world, and we know that we continue to battle with the flesh. We are tempted to shrink back in fear rather than share the gospel. We are tempted to harbor bitterness toward other Christians rather than view them as Jesus does. At times we are downright lousy ambassadors.

But thanks be to God that the ministry of reconciliation applies to us far beyond our initial conversion. We are reconciled to God, fellow heirs with Christ, and therefore we call out for mercy and help as we work for reconciliation with others in the world. We cannot and should not attempt this walk and calling in our own strength. Our boast is in Christ, who gives us the faith, grace, and strength to do what he asks of us. We are ambassadors, becoming reconcilers, motivated by love and the fear of the Lord (v. 11).

Engaging Confidently with Culture Today

Christians can engage confidently in the work of reconciliation because our confidence isn't in the flesh. We know that we can never do anything apart from Jesus. As Kristen reminds us in her chapter, our allegiance isn't to worldly structures and systems but to the Lord. This reality frees us to labor for our neighbor, to engage in the culture for the good of society, and to speak the truth in love.

One thing I have heard often is that people are afraid to engage on topics like ethnic pride, racial bias, racial profiling, and the sin of partiality because they do not want to offend. Perhaps they've previously made a mistake in their language that caused offense. And I hear that. I wish we were all more careful with our words, myself included. But speaking the truth in love means speaking truthfully and listening charitably. Only then can we begin to identify and address the pitfalls of racism in systems, people, and our own hearts.

There have been times of passion and anger when I've failed to engage with grace, and I regret those. I remember a time when a man made a derogatory comment on one of my social media posts. Although I am typically levelheaded and careful, I allowed my weariness to get the best of me, and I shot back at him. I can't remember my exact words, but I know I attempted to make him feel small and foolish. It worked, but it did not feel as good as I thought it would. I knew he was wrong, and he eventually realized it too. But the damage was done. He never engaged with me on the topic again, and I imagine he never will.

Engaging in the culture takes courage and risk, but also grace and forbearance. We want to speak the truth, but with the understanding that we don't know what the person we're speaking to has been through or experienced. This is the same posture we hope others would take with us.

When it comes to race, I have made an effort to assume that most people may not have been exposed to biblical teaching on the subject and may simply be ignorant of both the social aspects of the topic as well as the biblical principles. I don't want to come in with the assumption that everyone I engage with is more aware of these issues than they actually are. If we assume someone may simply not know, it allows for greater understanding and patience as we engage.

Another aspect we can remember when engaging in the culture, one that helps us engage confidently, is that we know the end: God, the ultimate Reconciler, is returning and making all things new. Remembering this truth allows me to rest in my heart, confident that one day all the confusion will end. God is going to wipe it all away: pain, sorrow, confusion, discouragement—and the sin of racism. I can rejoice knowing that sin has an expiration date. I can press into hard situations and conversations with grace because I know the end of the story.

If the ultimate goal is to speak the truth in love, I must evaluate my heart. Do I love the people I'm engaged with? Do I long to see them flourishing in the Lord, or do I simply wish to be right? If they've said something hurtful, am I working toward forgiveness?

We must remember that seeking to be reconcilers within the church is important to Christians because our love for one another testifies to the world about Jesus (John 13:35). So when we think about the world and engaging culture, we should not only think "out there." How we engage with one another on these topics is important. If the church is divided on race—and it is—what does that say to the world about us? How we seek to reconcile with one another could mean spiritual life or death to others looking in. It's important, and we shouldn't take this call lightly.

Fear Paralyzes Our Engagement

One of the biggest challenges hindering us from speaking confidently in the culture is fear. We can be paralyzed by fear of being misunderstood, fear of offending, and fear of appearing a certain way. Unfortunately, we can also fear that our association with Jesus will bring us harm rather than good.

The apostle Peter suffered from that paralyzing fear. We see the story chronicled in Luke 22:31–34. Jesus prophesized to Peter that Peter would deny him three times. A few verses later, Peter does just that. It took him no time at all to distance himself from his friend and soon-to-be crucified Lord. Peter was given three chances to redeem himself. Instead, he lied three times. He was not willing to go to prison with Jesus. He was not willing to follow the Way.

We, too, may be given the opportunity to stand up for what Jesus believed and taught us, or to deny him. We may be given a few of our own chances. What we will need to ask ourselves is whether we are going to bow to our fears or trust the living God.

Serving and working in areas of racial reconciliation and harmony have exposed me to a greater amount of vitriol and blatant racism than I imagine I would have experienced had I never begun communicating on social platforms or traveling to speak. I remember the first time an alt-right white supremacist harassed me online. Part of me wasn't surprised because of the general atmosphere in the country and the nature of social media. And yet another part of me felt gripped by hopelessness and fear. What if that anonymous attacker was actually a member of my church or a parent at one of my kids' schools? I had to wrestle with what I believed about God, what I knew about people, and to what God had called me.

Then and many times since, I have had to fight fear and trust God to work in and through me. Modeling this kind of engagement has required leaning on the power of the Spirit, crying out in prayer, and learning to discern when I need to speak and when to be silent. In many ways, for me, it's meant staying close to God. It has also meant seeking the input of others.

Here is a short list of ways the Lord has led me to practically engage.

1. Pray

Almost every word I say and write is preceded by prayer. That doesn't mean I always get it right! But prayer has helped me be at peace with what I've decided to engage, specifically on the topic of race. Prayer has also helped me to love my neighbor. It's hard to hate a person you've been praying for, and sometimes it is only prayer that keeps me from despairing. God does miraculous work on our hearts when we submit our pains and sorrows to him. When Jesus said we could do nothing apart from him, he meant it. Prayer acknowledges our weakness and utter dependence on the Lord. Self-sufficiency in ministry is a temptation, and frankly, we should not try to attempt the ministry of reconciliation without the Lord.

2. Be Slow to Speak

One way to do more harm than good in any situation is to be quick to speak and slow to listen. I have been especially aware of this recently in the aftermath of "breaking news"—when yet another tragedy occurs, everyone jumps in to comment.

Reporters try to get the information of an event out quickly, which means they often report before they have all the information. We do well to keep that in mind when we engage about those events—being slower to assume we know all the facts and slower to speak from our limited knowledge or, worse, our assumptions.

For example, when we hear that a police officer has shot an unarmed black man, it is right and good to mourn the loss of life. We need to be careful, however, not to immediately assume either that "That man should have obeyed the officer's commands!" or "That officer is a racist." As the full facts emerge, we may indeed find it necessary to speak out, but jumping in to comment prematurely rarely serves the cause of reconciliation. Think of the impact it would have on our culture if we first mourned with those who mourn.

We also want to be slow to speak when engaging person-to-person. Assuming a posture of learning and listening will not only serve the person who is sharing, but we will also have a greater opportunity to respond clearly and effectively. Anytime I've assumed I know what someone will say or what he or she is thinking, it's never ended well for me. I ended up needing to apologize. There's good reason that James instructs us to be slow to speak (James 1:19). Our slowness is an act of loving our neighbor as ourselves.

Another part of being slow to speak is discerning whether to speak at all. Not every statement or event requires an outward response from you and from me. We need to ask the Lord for discernment over what is important to engage on and what requires greater thought and prayer. There are certainly times when not speaking up would be irresponsible, depending on your role and calling. But for most of us, waiting and praying may be the best option.

3. Seek Out Real Relationships for Accountability and Support

I am not on an island by myself. I'm not trying to live out my faith and ministry alone. I am plugged in to a local church where I meet with people regularly. I am affiliated with an organization where colleagues offer me accountability and support. My husband is a friend and accountability partner in ministry. I share my life with people who can and do help me as I engage with the culture around me.

In our culture, individualism and isolation are the way many operate and live. But I have found that I simply can't function well without being part of a community that offers both accountability and support. Without accountability, I could easily forget the mission to which God has called me or fall into a trap of unhelpful and ungodly interactions. Without support, I could easily become a cynical and despairing person. Being involved with others strengthens my sense of calling and helps me remember that I'm ultimately accountable to God—and deeply loved by him.

Being involved in a local church body, especially, helps me remember that neighbor love and cultural engagement start at home. To a person who is often engaged in hard topics, it's refreshing to remember that there is life beyond the culture wars.

Reconciliation—true reconciliation—takes effort beyond simply saying sorry or even "Can't we all get along?" It takes dying to self, resisting apathy, evaluating where reparations might be made, and pursuing vulnerable relationships. Being a reconciler means extending grace and being open to others in ways that are often painful and costly.

Reconciliation is not easy. And it doesn't happen quickly. God's work to reconcile us to one another will require not only our participation but also our patience. It might take until Jesus returns for that reconciliation to be complete. But it will be worth it in the end. The final reconciliation that Jesus brings will be of such remarkable glory as to make the pain and hardship of our labor and longing seem as insignificant as a passing shadow. And in that hope, we can face the fractures of our world as the reconcilers we are called to be.

THE PEACEMAKER

CLAUDE RICHARD ALEXANDER JR.

"Blessed are the peacemakers, for they
will be called children of God."

—Matthew 5:9

WHILE ATTENDING SUNDAY SCHOOL AS A CHILD, MY CLASS-
mates and I were asked to memorize Bible verses. We began with single
verses, and over time worked up to memorizing several verses and
entire passages. Among them were Psalm 23, Psalm 100, the Lord's
Prayer, and the Beatitudes. Over the course of my life since, I have
been encouraged, inspired, convicted, and challenged by each of these
sections of Scripture. In the past ten years, however, none has challenged me more than the Beatitudes.

In Matthew 5, Jesus outlines the character expectations for all who
follow him. His followers will be blessed when they manifest certain
characteristics. In the first four characteristics—being poor in spirit,
mournful, meek, and hungering and thirsting after righteousness—
there is a recognition of need. With these come the promised blessings
of the kingdom of God: the comfort of God coming alongside you to

address the matter at hand, inheriting the earth, and being filled with and by God. Jesus then describes the characteristics that flow out of being filled with and by God as being merciful and pure in heart. The corresponding promised blessings are those of obtaining mercy and seeing God. Then there is one final blessing: those who shall be called the children of God. This comes to the peacemakers.

Jesus relies on two powerful understandings of peace. The Old Testament Hebrew word for peace is *shalom*.[1] It means wholeness, well-being, the presence of that which is good and positive. It alludes to the fullness of life that causes contentment. The New Testament Greek word is *eirene*.[2] It, too, speaks to the notion of well-being in contrast to evil of any sort. It also speaks to being in a state of rest and being undisturbed.

This well-being, this state of rest and wholeness, comes from God, in whom peace resides. Absolute and eternal, God is whole and undisturbed in himself. Creation at first reflected that wholeness, that well-being. Everything was good in and of itself. The natural world was at rest. Humanity was at rest. Adam and Eve were at rest within themselves, with each other, and with God.

This essential state of wholeness and well-being was disrupted by the fall. With the fall, unrest entered every level of the created world. Yet God remained at peace with himself and set in motion the means by which peace would be made within his creation. In Judges 6:23–24, God spoke peace to Gideon, who then built an altar and named it Yahweh Shalom ("the Lord is peace"). The sons of Korah testified of God's peace in Psalm 85:8, saying, "Let me hear what God the LORD will speak, for he will speak peace to his people, to his faithful."

This peace of God is invincible and all-excelling. Paul speaks of it as surpassing all understanding (Phil. 4:7). It is a well-being in the midst of the inconceivable, the unimaginable, and the unexplainable.

It is the state of being that led H. G. Spafford, while traveling across the Atlantic to claim the bodies of his four daughters who died in a ship accident, to write the words, "When peace like a river attendeth my way; when sorrow like sea billows roll. Whatever my lot, Thou hast taught me to say; It is well. It is well with my soul."[3]

However, Jesus did not say, "Blessed are the peace recipients." He did not say, "Blessed are the peace lovers." Having experienced God making peace with us and within us, Jesus called us to be peace *makers*.

We can also see the significance of peacemaking in the order in which Jesus established the Beatitudes. If we are not meek, we will never take responsibility for making peace. We will see ourselves as entitled to peace being made with us, not peace being made by us. We will expect peace to be made for us, not by us. But where there is humility before God, and a recognition of God's merciful action to reconcile us unto himself, there is the willingness to take responsibility and initiative in bringing peace and making peace with others.

The blessing for the peacemakers is the seventh beatitude. Seven is the biblical number for completion. In the very ordering of these Beatitudes, might Jesus have been suggesting that the Christian life is not complete until peacemaking is actively engaged? The complete life of the believer is seen in what the believer makes and makes happen. Christ-followers are not called to consume; they are called to contribute. They are not identified by what is made for them; they are identified by what they make. This is especially true when it comes to peace. God constantly challenges his people to be makers of peace. In Psalm 34:14, there is the admonition, "Depart from evil, and do good; seek peace, and pursue it." In Jeremiah 29:7, the Lord told the exiles in Babylon, "But seek the welfare of the city where I have sent you into exile."

The call to individual peacemaking is a call to accept responsibility for making peace. As such, the call is to see ourselves as personally responsible for working toward peace being felt and found. It is accepting the individual command to live and interact in a way that leads to wholeness and well-being.

The call to peacemaking is, therefore, also a call to take initiative. Christ-followers are not to wait for peace to be made. We are to work at making peace. The word for peacemakers literally means "peace bringers." This means that peacemakers must be willing to take the first step to establish peace.

In a society characterized by noise, strife, turmoil, unrest, violence, and unease, the call to peacemaking is also a call to make cultural peace. Christ-followers are to allow the peace within us to infect and influence our environment, to intentionally reflect and relay God's peace to others. As Etty Hillesum notes, "Ultimately, we have just one moral duty: to reclaim large areas of peace in ourselves, more and more peace, and to reflect it towards others. And the more peace there is in us, the more peace there will also be in our troubled world."[4]

We are admonished in Hebrews 12:14 to "pursue peace with everyone, and the holiness without which no one will see the Lord." We are to chase after peace as if in a hunt for it. Peacemaking is work and effort. It is work to establish right relationships with and between people, to live with and among others in such a way that they are more at rest, more at ease, in your presence than away from you.

This call to peacemaking is not a call to evade or avoid issues, but to face them, deal with them, and overcome them. Peacemaking calls us to address the forces and factors behind unrest, unease, and lack of well-being. Making peace and striving for justice are intimately entwined. Inequity and unfairness make communities and even nations rife with tension, hostility, and violence. Bringers of peace, therefore, cannot avoid issues of inequity, unfairness, and injustice. This means entering the fray to ensure equity in education, in housing, in employment. It means displaying solidarity in standing up against unfair treatment and excessive force by law enforcement. It means asserting the dignity of the image of God in all persons, advocating for the equal treatment under the law of all persons, and redressing wrongs perpetrated against any person.

Peacemaking is also countercultural. In a world where competition rules, Jesus calls his followers to live cooperatively. Eugene Peterson translates Matthew 5:9 this way: "You're blessed when you can show people how to cooperate instead of compete or fight" (THE MESSAGE). Jesus spoke these words to those who were experiencing marginalization and subjugation under Roman occupation. In such a context, these words were—and are—astonishing.

Yet peacemaking is not only between individuals and between cultures. Peacemaking is also internal. We can't come to terms with others if we haven't come to terms with ourselves. Hence, peacemaking requires a keen understanding of the unresolved issues within us so that we can overcome our woundedness and then offer and establish wholeness for and with others. The first person with whom you must make peace is yourself. It is only then that you can make peace with others.

This has been a challenge for me throughout my life. In 1970, I was a second grader in Jackson, Mississippi, where racism was still very much an issue. My mom and I had moved to Jackson from Washington, DC, in 1969, and she married the man who raised me. To avoid some of the desegregation challenges and to take advantage of the excellent programs in the Catholic school system, my parents enrolled me in one of the Catholic schools. I was the only person of color in my class. It was there that I was first called the N-word. I didn't know the word or what it meant. I knew only that the tone my classmate used was offensive and that the other kids, who were white, laughed. To say that I was wounded would be an understatement.

The feelings of isolation, hurt, embarrassment, and even betrayal were profound. Prior to that day and experience, I had thought that the classmate who called me that word was my friend. When I went home and told my mother about the day, her face held an unforgettable mixture of anger, sadness, and perplexity.

What she had tried to shield me from was unavoidable. How, she wondered, would she explain not just the term but the reality behind it in a way that would begin to ease my pain, bolster my self-esteem, provide me courage to continue, and quiet my rage? In her explanation, she sought to preserve an assumed naïveté on behalf of my classmate, saying that he was using a word he heard from others, but whose meaning he probably didn't know. She talked about racism and how it was not a reflection of me but of the people who held those views. She read to me about Dr. Martin Luther King Jr. As wise as her response was, I can't say that her words eliminated all of the pain and anger. I still faced an internal fight to see my inherent value, as well as to view my classmate and those who laughed in a positive vein.

I was awakened to racism and the devastating effects of being the only person of color in a hostile environment. At the age of seven, I had to find strategies for emotional and psychological survival as well as academic achievement. One such strategy was an active imagination. I noticed that my classmates liked the animated television series *Johnny Quest*. Johnny's best friend was Haji, one of the few characters of color on any cartoon. As a seven-year-old, I didn't see Haji as Indian; I saw him as colored like me. So I told my classmates that Haji was my cousin. And immediately I was accepted. The subtle but powerful message was that proximity to Haji made me acceptable. Haji wasn't seen as the ordinary person of color; he was extra-colored, you might say. And my acceptance was based on my proximity to someone viewed as exceptionally colored. This is the pressure placed even today upon many persons of color, particularly African Americans: that of having to be exceptional just to be seen and treated as equal.

I survived that year and was placed in a primarily black Catholic elementary school. I then went on to a racially mixed Catholic middle school and high school. In high school, I was reunited with my second-grade classmate. While neither of us ever mentioned the episode, I remembered it. Having reconciled myself both to his probable ignorance at the time and to my inherent worth and value, he and I would be cordial. Later on, I would have his support, as well as that of many of the kids who laughed in the second grade, to become the first person of color elected student body vice president.

The second experience of overcoming wounding occurred over a period of years with my biological father. My birth parents divorced when I was two. My father was only remotely involved during my childhood. In my teens, I began to question his lack of support. While I would hear from and receive birthday and Christmas greetings from my paternal grandmother and aunt, I received nothing from him. At the time, my father was gainfully employed as a technical writer for a defense contractor in the metro DC area. I eventually prompted my mother to take legal action to receive child support. To me, it wasn't a matter of need. It was a matter of principle. I was his only child. The legal proceedings meant I had to appear for a court hearing during the summer of 1979. I was fifteen, going into eleventh grade. On the day of the hearing, I found myself standing in the hall outside of the courtroom, two feet from my father. He did not recognize me.

Although it had been two years since we had been together, I had not substantially changed in appearance. During the proceeding, I sat in a daze at how surreal this was. I couldn't believe that my birth father, whose name I bore, not only did not recognize me but was resistant to the notion of providing any degree of support for his son. In the end, nothing substantive came of the legal process. The following school year I experienced immense depression, to the point of suicidal thoughts. I wrote a letter to my father expressing my pain. I never received a response.

During this time, God was revealing to me a call to ministry. Fortunately, I had the support of a high school English teacher, my pastor, and two uncles who were also pastors. They helped me discern God's voice. That process made God's love, care, and purpose tangibly real to me.

During the summer of 1982, while serving as a congressional intern in Washington, my paternal grandmother asked to have lunch with me. When we met, she informed me that my father had remarried and that she and my father wanted me to meet his new family. I sat there with a mixture of shock, anger, and sadness that my father neither considered contacting me prior to remarrying nor had the courage to tell me himself. I agreed to meet with them the following evening, yet throughout the night and well into the next day, an internal battle raged. To proceed or to cancel, to be belligerent or to be conciliatory: these were the polarities that tumbled through my eighteen-year-old mind. That evening, as I drove toward my grandmother's house, something unnatural or supernatural took place. A calm came over me. When I entered my grandmother's house, I was greeted by my father's wife, a strikingly beautiful woman bearing a nervous smile. She and I immediately clicked. She was fun-loving and happy-go-lucky. I was then introduced to her three children, with whom I would later bond. Over the course of the next eight years, this new family would serve as the means by which my relationship with my birth father would be repaired. And that reconciliation would be crucial as he eventually separated from his wife and fell into bad health. In 2008, he moved to Charlotte, where he lived until his death in July 2013.

Other experiences have also forced me to overcome wounding and to make peace. On more occasions than I'd like to count, instances of overt and covert racism have afflicted me and those whom I love. There are still times where I am followed by security when I am in a store, and when I am assumed to be the hired help by whites when staying at a resort. I wish those experiences were limited to the United States. Regrettably, they are not. On a recent layover in London, I went to an airline club where I have executive status. After presenting my Club Card, my passport, and showing my digital boarding pass, I requested a paper boarding pass. It wasn't an unusual request. It's one I've made many times. What was unusual was the interrogation I experienced. I was asked from whence I came, my means of transportation, what I do, where I work, who my supervisor is, and who my immediate subordinate is.

As I was going through this, I saw no one else being asked similar questions as they checked in and asked for a paper boarding pass. I held my peace, got my documents, and found a seat in the club. As I settled down, a question came to mind: Is there any place other than Africa and the Caribbean where I can go and not be seen as an N-word? Were it not for the gospel of Jesus Christ, it would be easy for me in my anger to be radicalized. When I think about all of this, it is clear that overcoming wounds and bringing and making peace can only be the result of a supernatural encounter with Christ. The natural response to being wounded is to wound in return. It is to preserve yourself by either attacking or disengaging from the person(s) who inflicted the wound. It is counterintuitive to desire the positive good and well-being of a person or people who have been hurtful to you. It requires a moral courage and a spiritual strength to defy the pull of bitterness and the desire for recrimination. My relationship with Christ has provided the means through which the hurt, sorrow, and anger have been overcome. It has been through him that I have been able to defy the pull to bitterness and seek the positive good and bring peace. The revelation of Christ as the One who "has borne our infirmities and carried our diseases" (Isa. 53:4) has provided the necessary balm to my heart, mind, and spirit. His love for me is what constrains and propels me toward the making of peace in the city of Charlotte and in the world.

For those who rise to the challenge of bringing peace, there is the promise that they will "be called children of God" (1 John 3:1). The word *called* means to be acknowledged and recognized. The promise to the peacemaker is that of being acknowledged as a child of God. Children reflect their parents physically and with their attitudes. In November 2017, the world was captivated by a video of a ten-year-old who used his face to unlock his mother's iPhone X, which had Face ID. The boy looked enough *like* his mother that he was seen *as* his mother. God desires for us to look enough like God for the world to see God.

The reflection of God is not solely through our worship. Worship is the activity of God's creation in response to him. We reflect God through the pursuit of the things that he pursues and our demonstrating his character in the world. Through the bringing and making of peace, we demonstrate and reflect the nature and character of God the Father.

That was the case when Nadine Collier, the daughter of Ethel Lance and the sister of Myra Thompson, brought peace to Charleston, South Carolina, by extending forgiveness to Dylann Roof.[5] Having suffered the most horrific of losses at the hands of Roof, whose explicitly racist motivations put the city of Charleston, as well as the nation, on edge, these family members, along with others, chose to bring peace through forgiveness rather than incite hostility through anger. Their doing so reflected the nature and character of God. And they were recognized as the children of God.

God himself also acts as peacemaker. He does so because he sees himself in the peacemaker. God is the God of peace. Peace comes from God. And in peacemakers God also sees a reflection of his Son, the only begotten of the Father. God sees the One whom Isaiah foretold: "For a child has been born for us, a son given to us; authority rests upon his shoulders; and he is named Wonderful Counselor, Mighty God, Everlasting Father, Prince of Peace. His authority shall grow continually, and there shall be endless peace for the throne of David and his kingdom. He will establish and uphold it with justice and with righteousness from this time onward and forevermore" (Isa. 9:6–7).

The peace that Jesus brought took many forms. He brought environmental peace. In Mark 4:39, with the storm-tossed sea threatening the lives of his disciples, Jesus rose from sleep and told the winds and the waves, "Peace! Be still!" Jesus also brought existential peace. In Mark 5:1–15, he encountered a man vexed by a multitude of demons, at war with himself, at odds with his community, and given to both self and societal destruction. Jesus called the demons out of him and transformed the man into one seated, at ease, at rest, "clothed and in his right mind."

Jesus spoke of this peace as his peace. To a room of disciples filled with unrest, Jesus said, "Peace I leave with you; my peace I give to you. I do not give to you as the world gives. Do not let your hearts be troubled, and do not let them be afraid" (John 14:27). Later, Jesus told them, "I have said this to you, so that in me you may have peace. In the world you face persecution. But take courage; I have conquered the world!" (John 16:33).

Most of all, Jesus brought eternal peace. Through his death and resurrection, we have the assurance of Romans 5:1–2: "Therefore, since we are justified by faith, we have peace with God through our Lord Jesus Christ, through whom we have obtained access to this grace in which we stand."

It is through Christ that you and I can heed the call to peacemaking. Paul provided the ground for our peacemaking and the glorious promise of it in Ephesians 2:14–18:

For he is our peace; in his flesh he has made both groups into one and has broken down the dividing wall, that is, the hostility between us. He has abolished the law with its commandments and ordinances, that he might create in himself one new humanity in place of the two, thus making peace, and might reconcile both groups to God in one body through the cross, thus putting to death that hostility through it. So he came and proclaimed peace to you who were far off and peace to those who were near; for through him both of us have access in one Spirit to the Father.

As a result, we can go out with confidence and work to follow our Lord in making peace.

CONCLUSION

JOHN INAZU AND TIMOTHY KELLER

AS WE NOTED IN OUR INTRODUCTION, WE LIVE IN A CULTURE
that lacks a shared understanding of the common good. Beneath
our social, religious, and political disagreements lie different understandings of moral authority, human nature, and even perceptions
of reality. And, as the past few generations have shown, we will not
resolve these differences through pragmatic or rationalistic appeals.
What is "pragmatic" depends on your understanding of a good life.
What is "rational" presupposes answers to questions about the nature
of truth and of reason.[1]

These challenges are likely to increase. Many of us will confront
greater differences in our daily lives due to growing religious pluralism,
the increase in nonbelievers, rising income inequality, and migration
to cities and other densely populated areas. Others will retreat further
into our own enclaves and echo chambers. This latter challenge is
particularly acute online. Unless we make deliberate efforts to the
contrary, our online experiences will increasingly be shaped by groups
that reinforce unchallenged beliefs, by curated feeds that manipulate
our emotional presuppositions, and by stories and images that take us
quite literally to alternate realities.[2]

In this cultural context, some American Christians are experiencing deep disorientation. For centuries we lived in a society that put social pressure on people to go to church and that contained, broadly speaking, moral intuitions shaped by the Bible. That society is rapidly passing away. Some of that change is good: social pressures to conform to American Christian norms usually meant *white* American Christian norms, at best ignoring and at worst reinforcing racial and other injustices. The loss of an assumed moral consensus provides an opportunity to address significant blind spots in the American church. But it is also true that shared assumptions about morality and religion facilitated common language and practices that allowed the church to contribute to the good of society in ways that will be more difficult in the absence of those shared norms.

In the midst of these current and coming realities, Christians are called to live and act in the world in the confidence and hope of Jesus Christ. We are assured of "a future with hope" as we seek to love our neighbors for our common well-being (Jer. 29:7, 11). Indeed, we may find increased opportunities for meaningful witness. The church has more often been a faithful witness when it lacked political power than at times when it sought to control.

When we asked ten other Christians to write about how they were living out their faith in various cultural fields in our historical moment, we did not know what they would say. Now that they have spoken, we see themes that echo James Davison Hunter's call for "faithful presence."[3]

To understand the meaning of faithful presence, Hunter first explains what it is *not* by critiquing three common responses of the church to culture. He names them "Defensive Against" (which seeks Christian dominance over society by politics or other means), "Purity From" (which withdraws into protective enclaves), and "Relevant To" (which adapts to the priorities and values of the culture in an effort to win favor).[4] The Defensive Against strategy is one of takeover. It does not know how to humbly and critically affirm what is good in the culture even as it critiques it. The Purity From strategy isolates itself from the larger culture. Both preserve some historic beliefs and practices, but both fail to approach the world from a stance of love and service. The Relevant To strategy overly adapts to social trends, naively failing to understand the nature of culture and its tension points with the gospel. Hunter warns that the church that adopts these belligerence, withdrawal, or compromise approaches "will not flourish in itself nor serve" our common life together.[5]

What then are the corresponding positive practices of faithful presence? If we look back over the chapters in this volume, we see the authors not only avoiding each of these mistaken stances toward our society but also pointing toward alternative practices. What does faithful presence actually look like? Here are four practices that provide the beginning of an answer.

First, *Christians should not overidentify with any particular political party or platform.* This does not mean that it is wrong to be a Democrat or a Republican (or a political independent, or part of some other party). Part of living in the world means making responsible choices to live and work within human institutions. But Christians should also be wary of any identity that claims primacy over their identity in Christ. Kristen Deede Johnson points us to Augustine's *City of God*, which warns us not to identify the kingdom of God with any earthly *polis*. Kristen admits that as a younger woman "my Christian convictions and my political convictions were not . . .

integrated." Rather, they were "siloed from one another, each shaped by different influences."

This description applies to many Christians today. We live in an increasingly secular culture, one that brackets out belief in the transcendent and seeks to justify all actions within an "immanent frame."[6] The politics of both Left and Right depart, in different ways, from the biblical account of people as fallen but redeemable divine image bearers. But seldom do Christians who are swept along by progressive politics (as the Relevant To approach does) or conservative politics (as the Defensive Against approach does) see this or recognize that they have sealed off their biblical beliefs from their political views. Too often, these political views are rooted in an earthly *polis* rather than the City of God.

Relatedly, white American Christians will need to acclimate to a certain loss of power and privilege. Tom Lin's chapter provides a helpful perspective on this. As the child of Asian immigrants, he spent his younger years feeling "cultural dissonance," not really fitting in completely with either mainstream American or Asian culture. Then he came to see that *all* Christians should be living as "resident aliens" in *every* culture. Older, white American Christians in particular, we believe, can learn from the many younger, nonwhite Christian voices in the American church—and in the global church. Importantly, part of learning means surrendering control and demonstrating a willingness to be led by others. It means sharing resources and platforms, rather than assuming that old and familiar models of ministry will always be the right ones. In some segments of evangelical culture, this will mean rethinking longstanding institutional norms and assumptions.

Second, ***Christians should approach the community around them through a posture of love and service.*** While the Defensive Against strategy often focuses on regaining lost power, and the Purity

From strategy fears a loss of holiness from too much contact with the non-Christian world, the chapters in this book show Christians pouring themselves into their surrounding communities. Sara Groves shows how her community at Art House North in St. Paul, Minnesota, serves as an arts center for the entire neighborhood. It embodies her belief, gleaned from Mako Fujimura, that culture is a garden to be cultivated rather than a war to be won or lost. This approach will not always be easy. We may often have our engagement with the world regarded with suspicion. Rudy Carrasco found Harambee Ministries under suspicion from both secular community groups that were wary of its overtly Christian message and conservative Christian groups that disliked its justice orientation. But suspicion and distrust from others should not discourage us from the work to which we have been called.

Third, ***Christians should recognize that the gospel subverts rival stories and accounts of reality.*** As Hunter says, there is great danger in trying to adapt too much to the culture in an effort to be seen as relevant. When this happens, the gospel of God's unconditional love in Jesus is reduced to just another way to help individual self-esteem. Hunter says that this approach is ultimately superficial—it doesn't differentiate between the story of the world told in the Bible and other accounts of reality. Bible verses on justice can be turned into proof-texts for an identity politics that decenters our primary identity as followers of Jesus.

Tish Harrison Warren provides a case study. A university administration declared all Christian campus groups requiring a profession of biblical faith to be practicing "discrimination"—but claimed themselves to be objective, open, and inclusive of all views. Tish's commitment to writing with truth and compassion allowed her to show that to deny the importance of religious doctrine is itself a doctrine, a very particular view of truth and moral value that was being imposed. "Flattening differences" between religions was a denial of the very "robust pluralism" that the university claimed to be promoting.[7]

Lecrae's chapter explains how Christians can use the gospel as a counter-narrative to subvert the dominant stories in their communities yet fulfill their best longings as well. He outlines the competing stories told about police shootings of black youth. One narrative sees urban youth as victims of social forces and police as evildoers. The other reverses roles, making the police the victims of circumstance and the youth the villains. Lecrae responds that unlike all other storylines, the gospel reminds us that human beings are always simultaneously guilty sinners and God's image bearers. Actors on both sides of many of these incidents are often both victims of social forces *and* wrongdoers. Human heroism and villainy are always mixed, never pure. As Lecrae writes, "The one true hero is Jesus and his power to restore broken hearts and repair the infrastructures corrupted by sin."

The fourth practice, described more fully in the introduction, is that *Christians should reach out to others with humility, patience, and tolerance.* We see these relational principles embodied in Shirley Hoogstra's chapter on bridge building to find common ground across contentious policy differences, and in Trillia Newbell's and Claude Alexander's chapters on reconciliation and peacemaking. We can also see these ideas at work in Warren Kinghorn's introspection about his own family's complicity in injustice and his critique of his own psychiatric profession. The balance between openness to criticism and love and respect for those with opposing views stands out on every page of these stories.

How do Christians reach out across difference? How do we maintain our distinctiveness from the world, rather than merely blending in? How do we serve others, rather than self-protectively withdrawing?

We believe the stories in this book help show us the way forward. It begins with knowing who we are in Christ as we live "with all humility and gentleness, with patience, showing tolerance for one another in love" (Eph. 4:2 NASB).

ACKNOWLEDGMENTS

WE ARE GRATEFUL TO THE MANY PEOPLE WHO HELPED MAKE this book possible. Thanks first and foremost to our ten collaborators who shared with us not only their words and their time but also their trust. In addition, we are grateful to Boyd Bowman, Johanna Christophel, Andy Crouch, Craig Ellis, Allison Gaskins, John Hendrix, Matt Kile, Andy Kim, Mollie Moore, Carol Quinlan, Seth Reid, Alex Siemers, and Allie Spors. Thanks to Tim's agent, David McCormick, and to the team at Thomas Nelson, especially our editor, Webster Younce. We also thank Redeemer City-to-City, The Carver Project, and Washington University in St. Louis.

We are grateful to our families for their support and encouragement of this book: Kathy Keller, and Caroline, Lauren, Hana, and Sam Inazu.

This book is dedicated to John's father, Willie Inazu. A few weeks before we launched this project with a gathering of the authors, Willie was diagnosed with terminal lung cancer. His illness and death coincided with the writing and editing of this book. Willie died a free man. Free of unnecessary pain, having courageously chosen hospice. A free citizen, who devoted his life in service to this country despite having been born a prisoner at Manzanar Internment Camp in 1943. And free of guilt and regret, having faith in things to come.

NOTES

Introduction

1. Parts of this introduction draw from John Inazu and Timothy Keller, "How Christians Can Bear Gospel Witness in an Anxious Age," *Christianity Today*, June 20, 2016.

2. E.g., John Rawls, "The Idea of an Overlapping Consensus," *Oxford Journal of Legal Studies* 7, no. 1 (1987): 4.

3. See Jemar Tisby, *The Color of Compromise: The Truth About the American Church's Complicity in Racism* (Grand Rapids, MI: Zondervan, 2019).

4. James Davison Hunter, *To Change the World: The Irony, Tragedy, and Possibility of Christianity in the Late Modern World* (Oxford: Oxford University Press, 2010), 95.

5. For an account of the decline of the mainline Protestant influence on white middle-class America and the failure of either evangelicalism or Roman Catholicism to replace that influence, see Joseph Bottum, *An Anxious Age: The Post-Protestant Ethic and the Spirit of America* (New York: Random House, 2014).

6. As Luke Bretherton has noted, "Under conditions of a fallen and finite political life, the idea that there can be an all-encompassing common good is highly problematic. Determining the common good of a family, workplace, or small-scale community is possible and, arguably, necessary, for politics of the kind I outline here to be achievable. But beyond that scale, a claim to know the common good

of a conurbation, region, nation, or the globe is antipolitical. It denies the plurality and contestability of moral visions in complex societies and the conflicts that arise in pursuit of divergent moral goods, all of which must be negotiated through politics." Luke Bretherton, *Christ and the Common Life: Political Theology and the Case for Democracy* (Grand Rapids, MI: Wm. B. Eerdmans, 2019), 32, n.13.

7. John D. Inazu, *Confident Pluralism: Surviving and Thriving Through Deep Difference* (Chicago: University of Chicago Press, 2016).

8. Thanks to Andy Crouch for making the connection for us in this way.

9. Lesslie Newbigin put it this way: "We are continually required to act on beliefs that are not demonstrably certain and to commit our lives to propositions that can be doubted." Lesslie Newbigin, *Proper Confidence: Faith, Doubt, and Certainty in Christian Discipleship* (Grand Rapids, MI: Wm. B. Eerdmans, 1995), 102.

10. As Mark Lilla points out, the Christian hope in a future restoration of all things avoids both the utopianism of liberalism and the pessimistic nostalgia of conservatism. Mark Lilla, *The Shipwrecked Mind: On Political Reaction* (New York: New York Review Books, 2016), 67–85.

11. Sherry Turkle, *Reclaiming Conversation: The Power of Talk in a Digital Age* (New York: Penguin, 2015). See her chapter "The Empathy Diaries" on pages 2–28, but also throughout.

12. Flannery O'Connor, "Writing Short Stories" in *Mystery and Manners* (New York: Farrar, Straus and Giroux, 1970), 96.

The Theologian: Kristen Deede Johnson

1. Bethany Hanke Hoang and I explored the idea that we are called to be saints, not heroes, in *The Justice Calling: When Passion Meets Perseverance* (Grand Rapids, MI: Baker, 2016), 111–38.

2. Samuel Wells, *Improvisation: The Drama of Christian Ethics* (Grand Rapids, MI: Brazos Press, 2004), 44.

3. James Davison Hunter, *To Change the World: The Irony, Tragedy, and Possibility of Christianity in the Late Modern World* (Oxford: Oxford University Press, 2010).

4. Hunter describes this as the adoption of Nietzschean categories of

the will to power and *ressentiment* that have made anger and winning the driving forces behind much public Christian engagement. See James Davison Hunter, *To Change the World: The Irony, Tragedy, and Possibility of Christianity in the Late Modern World* (Oxford: Oxford University Press, 2010).
5. See Amy E. Black, *Honoring God in Red or Blue: Approaching Politics with Humility, Grace, and Reason* (Chicago, IL: Moody Publishers, 2012).

The Pastor: Timothy Keller

1. "The Age of Authenticity" in Charles Taylor, *A Secular Age* (Cambridge, MA: Harvard University Press, 2007), 473–504.
2. Charles Taylor, *Sources of the Self: The Making of Modern Identity* (Cambridge, MA: Harvard University Press, 1989).
3. *The New English Bible* (Oxford University Press and Cambridge University Press, 1970), 54.
4. Hugh McLeod et al., *The Decline of Christendom in Western Europe, 1750–2000* (Cambridge, UK: Cambridge University Press, 2003), 1, cited in Stefan Paas, "Challenges and Opportunities in Doing Evangelism" in *Sharing Good News: Handbook on Evangelism in Europe*, ed. G. Noort, K. Avtzi, and S. Pass (Geneva, Switzerland: World Council of Churches, 2017), 38.
5. Jennifer Senior argues that in a transactional, individualistic culture, children "are the last binding obligation in a culture that asks for almost no other permanent commitments at all." Jennifer Senior, *All Joy and No Fun: The Paradox of Modern Parenthood* (New York: HarperCollins, 2014), 44.
6. See Dan Piepenbring, "Chick-Fil-A's Creepy Infiltration of New York City," *New Yorker*, April 13, 2018, https://www.newyorker.com /culture/annals-of-gastronomy/chick-fil-as-creepy-infiltration-of-new -york-city.
7. See Carl Trueman's great short essay "Blessing When Cursed" in *First Things*, June 14, 2019, https://www.firstthings.com/web-exclusives /2019/06/blessing-when-cursed. Trueman was addressing a call by some conservatives to abandon "politeness, respect, and decency" in

their controversy with secular opponents. Carl rightly reminds us that Christians are called to speak in this way not because it works but because "it is the right way to reflect the character of God to the world."

The Adventurer: Tom Lin

1. Lesslie Newbigin, *The Open Secret: An Introduction to the Theology of Mission* (Grand Rapids, MI: Wm. B. Eerdmans, 1995), 5.
2. Samuel E. Escobar, *The New Global Mission: The Gospel from Everywhere to Everyone* (Downers Grove, IL: IVP Academic, 2003), 19–20.
3. John Inazu, "Do Black Lives Matter to Evangelicals?" *Washington Post*, January 6, 2016.
4. Melinda Lundquist Denton and Christian Smith, *Soul Searching: The Religious and Spiritual Lives of American Teenagers* (Oxford, UK: Oxford University Press, 2005).
5. J. R. R. Tolkien, *The Return of the King* (New York: Del Ray/Ballantine Books, 2001), 338.

The Entrepreneur: Rudy Carrasco

1. Randy Otterbridge, *Reluctant Entrepreneur: Going from Fear to First Steps Toward Starting Your Own Business* (Grand Rapids, MI: R&A Publishing, 2012).
2. Anthony Bradley, "You Are the Manure of the Earth," *Christianity Today*, September 23, 2016.
3. Vicki Torres, "Tension Takes a Toll: Feuding Gangs, Drive-by Killings Spread Fear in Pasadena Area," *Los Angeles Times*, February 2, 1991, https://www.latimes.com/archives/la-xpm-1991–02–02-me-169-story .html.
4. Daniela Perdomo, "Pasadena Gang Violence Raises Fears," *Los Angeles Times*, December 25, 2007, https://www.latimes.com/archives/la-xpm -2007-dec-25-me-race25-story.html.

The Writer: Tish Harrison Warren

1. As far as I can tell, she didn't actually say this. But it is a fair representation of her thought. Weil writes in her journals, for

instance: "Duration, whether it be a matter of centuries in the case of civilizations or of years and decades in the case of the human being, possesses a Darwinian function of elimination of the unfit. That which is fit for all purposes is eternal." Simone Weil, *The Notebooks of Simone Weil*, trans. Arthur Wills (New York: Routledge, 2004), 444.

2. Luci Shaw, *Breath for the Bones: Art, Imagination, and Spirit* (Nashville: Thomas Nelson, 2007), 87.

3. This phrasing was reported to me by my friend Robert Kehoe, who heard Hauerwas say this in an unpublished public lecture. And this is a consistent theme in Hauerwas's works: "What so often makes us liars is not what we do, but the justifications we offer for what we do. Our justifications become the way we try to defeat the contingencies of our lives by telling ourselves consoling stories that suggest we have done as well as was possible. . . . Being Christian means that I must try to make sense of my life in the light of the gospel, so I do not get to determine the truthfulness of my story. Rather, those who live according to the gospel will be the ones to determine where I have been truthful and where I have deceived myself." Stanley Hauerwas, *Hannah's Child: A Theologian's Memoir* (Grand Rapids, MI: Wm. B. Eerdmans, 2013), 159.

4. Nicholas Carr, *The Shallows: What the Internet Is Doing to Our Brains* (New York: W. W. Norton & Company, 2011), 7.

5. Thomas Merton, *The Sign of Jonas* (New York: Harcourt, Brace and Company, 1953), 266.

6. John Berger, *Hold Everything Dear: Dispatches on Survival and Resistance* (New York: Pantheon Books, 2007), 48.

7. Francis Spufford, *Unapologetic: Why, Despite Everything, Christianity Can Still Make Surprising Emotional Sense* (New York: HarperOne, 2013), 215.

The Songwriter: Sara Groves

1. Makoto Fujimura, *On Becoming Generative: An Introduction to Culture Care* (New York: Fujimura Institute and International Arts Movement, 2013). Digital. In this short pamphlet, Mako introduces

three Gs to guide his generative principals. Genesis: as found in creativity, both its growth and failure; Generosity: a gift that pushes back against utility and transactional ways of living; and Generational Thinking: "They grow in conversation with the past and in our intention to speak and create so as to cultivate the values of multiple future generations."

2. Makoto Fujimura, *Culture Care: Reconnecting with Beauty for Our Common Life* (Downers Grove, IL: InterVarsity Press, 2017).

3. Charlie Peacock, *A New Way to Be Human: A Provocative Look at What It Means to Follow Jesus* (Colorado Springs: WaterBrook Press, 2004), 93.

4. Sara Groves, "Why It Matters," *Add to the Beauty*, SG Music, 2005.

5. Sara Groves, "Any Comfort," (unrecorded).

6. Flannery O'Connor, *Mystery and Manners* (New York: Farrar, Straus and Giroux, 1970), 177.

7. O'Connor, *Mystery and Manners*, 44.

8. My paraphrase of Psalm 73:3–21.

9. My paraphrase of Psalm 73:22.

10. Sara Groves, "Like a Skin," *The Other Side of Something*, SG Music, 2004.

11. See http://fortune.com/2016/09/15/great-migration-racism-history/ for an interview with Pulitzer Prize–winning journalist Isabel Wilkerson on her book *The Warmth of Other Suns*, which captures in great detail the Great Migration and redlining practices in cities all across America.

12. Sara Groves, "Floodplain," *Floodplain*, SG Music, 2015.

13. Sara Groves, "In the Girl There's a Room," *Tell Me What You Know*, SG Music, 2007.

14. Sara Groves, "Eyes Wide Open," *Fireflies and Songs*, SG Music, 2009.

15. Sara Groves, "It's Me," *Fireflies and Songs*, SG Music, 2009.

The Storyteller: Lecrae

1. See Rachel Gillett, "How Walt Disney, Oprah Winfrey, and 19 Other Successful People Rebounded After Getting Fired," *Inc.*, October 7, 2015, https://www.inc.com/business-insider/21-successful-people-who -rebounded-after-getting-fired.html.

2. See Gillett, "How Walt Disney, Oprah Winfrey, and 19 Other Successful People Rebounded After Getting Fired."

The Translator: John Inazu

1. Ken Bain, *What the Best College Teachers Do* (Cambridge, MA: Harvard University Press, 2004), 174.

2. Lesslie Newbigin, *Proper Confidence: Faith, Doubt, and Certainty in Christian Discipleship* (Grand Rapids, MI: Wm. B. Eerdmans, 1995), 14.

3. Recently, some colleagues and I have worked to embody this work through a ministry called The Carver Project (carverstl.org), which exists to cultivate whole-life disciples at the intersection of university, church, and society.

4. Lecrae, "Facts," *All Things Work Together*, Columbia Records Group, 2017.

5. See, for example, my chapter responding to Eboo's arguments in Eboo Patel, *Out of Many Faiths: Religious Diversity and the American Promise* (Princeton, NJ: Princeton University Press, 2018). See also Doug Lederman, "A Call for 'Confident Pluralism' on Campuses," *Inside Higher Ed*, January 30, 2017 (profiling a public dialogue between Eboo and me to the annual meeting of the presidents of Christian colleges and universities).

The Bridge Builder: Shirley V. Hoogstra

1. Junno Arocho Esteves, "Pope Francis Washes Feet of Refugees on Holy Thursday," *Catholic Herald*, March 24, 2016, https://catholicherald.co.uk/news/2016/03/24/pope-francis-washes-feet-of-refugees-on-holy-thursday/.

The Caregiver: Warren Kinghorn

1. *Gantt v. Clemson Agric. Coll.*, 320 F.2d 611, 614 (4th Cir. 1963).

2. See, for example, Kelly M. Hoffman, Sophie Trawalter, Jordan R. Axt, and M. Norman Oliver, "Racial Bias in Pain Assessment and Treatment Recommendations, and False Beliefs about Biological Differences Between Blacks and Whites," *Proceedings of the National Academy of Sciences USA* 113, no. 16 (2016): 4296–301.

3. Sophia Haeri, "Disparities in Diagnosis of Bipolar Disorder in Individuals of African and European Descent: A Review," *Journal of Psychiatric Practice* 17 (2011): 394.

4. Allen Verhey and Warren Kinghorn, "'The Hope to Which He Has Called You': Medicine in Christian Apocalyptic Perspective," *Christian Bioethics* 22 (2016): 21–38.

5. Janice L. Krupnick et al., "The Role of the Therapeutic Alliance in Psychotherapy and Pharmacotherapy Outcome: Findings in the National Institute of Mental Health Treatment of Depression Collaborative Research Program," *Journal of Consulting and Clinical Psychology* 64 (1996): 532–39.

6. Curt Thompson, *The Soul of Shame: Retelling the Stories We Believe about Ourselves* (Downers Grove, IL: InterVarsity Press, 2015).

7. Wendell Berry, *The Hidden Wound* (Berkeley, CA: Counterpoint, 2010).

8. Josef Pieper, *Faith, Hope, Love* (San Francisco: Ignatius, 1997), 163–64.

The Reconciler: Trillia Newbell

1. Karen Grigsby Bates, "Rodney King Comes to Grips with 'the Riot Within,'" *NPR*, April 23, 2012, https://www.npr.org/2012/04/23/150985823/rodney-king-comes-to-grips-with-the-riot-within.

2. Marcy was not her real name; it has been changed for this chapter.

3. See John 4:9, 8:48, and Luke 9:51–56.

4. Trillia Newbell, *United: Captured by God's Vision for Diversity* (Chicago, IL: Moody Publishers, 2014).

The Peacemaker: Claude Richard Alexander Jr.

1. James Strong, *A Concise Dictionary of the Words in the Greek Testament and the Hebrew Bible*, vol. 2 (Bellingham, WA: Faithlife, 2009), 115.

2. Strong, *Concise Dictionary*, vol. 1 (Bellingham, WA: Faithlife, 2009), 25.

3. Kenneth W. Osbeck, *Amazing Grace: 366 Inspiring Hymn Stories for Daily Devotions* (Grand Rapids, MI: Kregel Publications, 1996), 202.

4. Etty Hillesum, *Etty Hillesum: An Interrupted Life; The Diaries, 1941–1943, and Letters from Westerbork*, trans. Arnold J. Pomerans (New York: Metropolitan Books, 1983), 218.

5. Elahe Izadi, "The Powerful Words of Forgiveness Delivered to Dylann Roof by Victims' Relatives," *Washington Post*, June 19, 2015, https://www.washingtonpost.com/news/post-nation/wp/2015/06/19/hate-wont-win-the-powerful-words-delivered-to-dylann-roof-by-victims-relatives/?noredirect=on&utm_term=.4c796b6af711.

Conclusion

1. See generally Alister E. McGrath, *The Territories of Human Reason: Science and Theology in an Age of Multiple Rationalities* (Oxford, UK: Oxford University Press, 2019); Lesslie Newbigin, *Proper Confidence: Faith, Doubt, and Certainty in Christian Discipleship* (Grand Rapids, MI: Wm. B. Eerdmans, 1995); and Alasdair MacIntyre, *Whose Justice? Which Rationality?* (Notre Dame, IL: University of Notre Dame Press, 1988) and *After Virtue: A Study in Moral Theory* (Notre Dame, IL: University of Notre Dame Press, 1981).

2. A striking example of alternative realities that shape online media is the emergence of "deep fakes." See Robert Chesney and Danielle Citron, "Deepfakes and the New Disinformation War: The Coming Age of Post-Truth Geopolitics," *Foreign Affairs* (January/February 2019). For guidance on practical steps that Christians can take to limit unhealthy online engagement, see Justin Whitmel Earley, *The Common Rule: Habits of Purpose for an Age of Distraction* (Downers Grove, IL: InterVarsity Press, 2019); Andy Crouch, *The Tech-Wise Family: Everyday Steps for Putting Technology in Its Proper Place* (Grand Rapids, MI: Baker Books, 2017); Tish Harrison Warren, *Liturgy of the Ordinary: Sacred Practices in Everyday Life* (Downers Grove, IL: InterVarsity Press, 2016).

3. James Davison Hunter, *To Change the World: The Irony, Tragedy, and Possibility of Christianity in the Late Modern World* (Oxford: Oxford University Press, 2010), 214–19.

4. When Lesslie Newbigin called the church in the post-Christendom West to a "missionary encounter with western culture" he first delineated what such an encounter was not. The three things it is not—dominance, assimilation, and withdrawal—align with Hunter's three wrong approaches to culture. See Lesslie Newbigin, *Foolishness to*

the Greeks (Grand Rapids, MI: Wm. B. Eerdmans, 1988), and Lesslie Newbigin, "Can the West Be Converted?" *International Bulletin of Missionary Research,* January 1987.

5. James Davison Hunter, *To Change the World: The Irony, Tragedy, and Possibility of Christianity in the Late Modern World* (Oxford: Oxford University Press, 2010), 285.

6. See Charles Taylor, *A Secular Age* (Cambridge, MA: Bellknap Press, 2007), for this now well-known description of our culture.

7. By styling itself as an absence of faith, secularity is doing something that cultural theorists have called "mystification." Terry Eagleton defines it this way: "It is taking a contestable viewpoint or belief and denigrating any views that challenge it, marginalizing all rival forms of thought, and denying the social reality that the belief is not universally held. This gives the opinion the appearance of being a universal, self-evident, inevitable fact that may not be questioned." Terry Eagleton, *Ideology: An Introduction* (New York: Verso, 1991), 5–6.

SELECTED WORKS BY CONTRIBUTORS

Books

Claude Richard Alexander Jr., *Necessary Christianity: Living a Must Life in a Maybe World* (MMGI Publishers House, 2013).

John Inazu, *Liberty's Refuge: The Forgotten Freedom of Assembly* (Yale University Press, 2012) and *Confident Pluralism: Surviving and Thriving Through Deep Difference* (University of Chicago Press, 2016).

Kristen Deede Johnson, *Theology, Political Theory, and Pluralism: Beyond Tolerance and Difference* (Cambridge University Press, 2010) and Kristen Deede Johnson and Bethany Hoang, *The Justice Calling: Where Passion Meets Perseverance* (Brazos Press, 2017).

Timothy Keller, *Generous Justice: How God's Grace Makes Us Just* (Viking, 2010), *The Prodigal God: Recovering the Heart of the Christian Faith* (Penguin Books, 2011), and *Making Sense of God: Finding God in the Modern World* (Penguin Books, 2018).

Lecrae, *Unashamed* (B&H Books, 2016).

Tom Lin, *Losing Face, Finding Grace: 12 Bible Studies for Asian-Americans* (InterVarsity Press, 1996).

Trillia Newbell, *Fear and Faith: Finding the Peace Your Heart Craves* (Moody Publishers, 2015) and *If God Is for Us: The Everlasting Truth of Our Great Salvation* (Moody Publishers, 2019).

Tish Harrison Warren, *Liturgy of the Ordinary: Sacred Practices in Everyday Life* (InterVarsity Press, 2016).

Discography

Sara Groves, *Tell Me What You Know* (INO, 2007) and *Floodplain* (Fair Trade, 2016).

Lecrae, *Gravity* (Reach, 2012) and *All Things Work Together* (Reach, 2017).